SKINNY VEGETARIAN ENTRÉES

SKINNY COOKING

Skinny Vegetarian

ENTRÉES

PHYLLIS MAGIDA
SUE SPITLER

SURREY BOOKS
CHICAGO

SKINNY VEGETARIAN ENTRÉES is published by Surrey Books, Inc.
230 E. Ohio St., Suite 120, Chicago, IL 60611.

Second edition: 1 2 3 4 5

This book is manufactured in the United States of America.

Library of Congress Cataloging-in-Publication data:

Magida, Phyllis.
    Skinny vegetarian entrées / Phyllis Magida and Sue Spitler—2nd ed.
    200p.   cm.
    Includes index.
    ISBN 1-57284-007-2 (pbk.)
    1. Vegetarian cookery.   2. Entrées (Cookery).   I. Spitler, Sue.
II. Title.
RM236.M34 1996
641.5'63—dc20   96-24481
                                                                    CIP

Editorial and production: *Bookcrafters, Inc., Chicago*
Art Director: *Joan Sommers Design, Chicago*
Cover and interior illustrations by *Mona Daly*

For free catalog and prices on quantity purchases, contact Surrey Books at the
address above.

This title is distributed to the trade by Publishers Group West.

Titles in the "Skinny" Cookbooks Series:

Skinny Beef	*Skinny Pasta*
Skinny Chicken	*Skinny Pizzas*
Skinny Chocolate	*Skinny Potatoes*
Skinny Comfort Foods	*Skinny Sandwiches*
Skinny Cookies, Cakes & Sweets	*Skinny Sauces & Marinades*
Skinny Grilling	*Skinny Seafood*
Skinny Italian Cooking	*Skinny Soups*
Skinny Mexican Cooking	*Skinny Spices*
Skinny One-Pot Meals	*Skinny Vegetarian Entrées*

Thank you...

cooking associate Cindy Roth for having chopped and simmered
your way through bushels of vegetables and bags of grains.
And thank you Brina Rodin for eating your way through giant
potfuls of vegetables as you tasted and commented on every dish.

CONTENTS

INTRODUCTION

Until a few years ago, vegetables were the last thing eaten on any-
body's plate. And often they weren't eaten at all. But that's all
changing today. Nutritionists tell us that to be healthy we must cut
down on high-fat, low-fiber animal protein and eat more low-fat, high-fiber
vegetables and grains. Conservationists urge us to eat vegetables rather
than meat so we don't have to cut down our precious rain forests to use as
grazing land.

Economists tell us that eating animals is unsound financially, that a
pound of beef costs as much as ten pounds of grain to produce. And
humanists tell us we've no moral right to kill and eat animals when there
are so many other, healthier food choices.

But few of us are interested in returning to the plain old over-boiled
vegetables of a few years back. And that's why we decided to write this

book—to create over 110 vegetable main dishes that are both delicious and healthy.

And they are. All of our entrees are full-flavored, from the lighter whole-meal salads and sandwiches to the heartier and more elaborate stews, casseroles, and pasta entrees.

It's often thought that vegetarian cooking must use strange ingredients, like wheat germ and tofu, or be high in fat due to ingredients such as nuts and cheese, which are included for nutritional reasons.

But when you look at these recipes and their nutritional breakdowns, you'll see that this just isn't true. Our recipes fall within American Heart Association guidelines: few entree portions exceed 500 calories or contain more than 125 mg of cholesterol and 800 mg of sodium. And none of the entrees exceeds the 30 percent of calories from fat guideline.

Specific nutritional information is provided for each recipe in this book, but please remember that nutritional data are rarely—if ever—infallible. The recipe analyses were derived using software highly regarded by nutritionists and dietitians. Figures are based on actual lab values of ingredients rather than general rules of thumb, such as each fat gram contains 9 calories, so our results might vary slightly from traditional formulas.

Other factors affecting the nutritional data include: the variable sizes of vegetables and fruits; a plus or minus 20 percent error factor on the nutritional labels of packaged foods; and cooking techniques and appliances. Thus, if you have any health problems that mandate strict dietary requirements, it is important to consult a physician, clinical dietitian, or nutritionist before proceeding with any recipe in this book. Also, if you are a diabetic or require a diet that restricts calories, fat, or sodium, remember that the nutritional analysis figures may be accurate for the recipe we tested but not for the food you cooked due to the variables.

Please also note that ingredients listed as "optional" or "to taste" or as "garnish" are not included in the nutritional data. When alternate choices of ingredients are given, the first-listed item is the one used to develop the nutritional data.

In summary, use the nutritional data as a starting point for planning healthier meals, but regard the figures more as guidelines than as components of an immutable formula.

Our recipes were created to accommodate all kinds of vegetarians: vegans, who eat no meat or dairy products; lacto-vegetarians, who do eat dairy but not eggs; ovo-vegetarians, who do eat eggs but not dairy; and lacto-ovo-vegetarians, who eat both eggs and dairy.

We've included recipes such as baked vegetables loaves and casseroles for family meals, recipes like three-foot-long veggie submarines for special events, and creations such as Cabbage-Fennel Strudel for more formal dining. Dishes range from quick-to-make, like the Frittata Pasta, to more complex stews and risottos, with deep, simmered flavors (try the Romanian

Stew with Red Wine and Grapes). We've even included some ultra-comfort foods for bad days and cold nights, like the Old Fashioned Corn, Tomato, and Cheese Pudding and our Black and White Bean Chili.

The ingredients we've used are readily available in supermarkets. In the few recipes that include unusual ingredients, you'll find instructions on how to obtain them. Herbs called for in recipes are in dried form unless stated otherwise; cilantro, garlic, and parsley are always used fresh. Ground spices are intended unless specifically stated as whole.

We want to stress that the recipes in this book are much like the foods you've always eaten. You'll find no weird ingredients or strange textures or flavors. What you will find are over 110 delicious vegetable entrees, including Boston Baked Beans and Brown Bread and All-Season Risotto and Spinach-Noodle Casserole and Grill-Roasted Vegetables with Polenta.

We hope you'll have as much fun making and eating these dishes as we did creating them for you.

Phyllis Magida and Sue Spitler

1
SOUPS

Everything-But-Cabbage Vegetable Soup

Cream of Fava Bean Soup

Split Pea Soup with 3 Accompaniments

Polish Style Mushroom-Barley-Vegetable Soup

Tomato Soup with Sour Cream and
4 Accompaniments

Roasted Vegetable Minestrone

EVERYTHING-BUT-CABBAGE VEGETABLE SOUP

Serves 4

6 cups canned low-sodium vegetable broth
3 ears corn, each cut in 3 pieces
3/4 cup ends-trimmed, cut (1/2 inch) green beans
2 tablespoons reduced-calorie margarine
3/4 cup minced onion
3 cups peeled, diced baking potatoes
3/4 cup peeled, diced carrots
3/4 cup peeled, diced celery
3/4 cup peeled, diced sweet potatoes
3/4 cup peeled, diced butternut squash
3/4 cup peeled, diced zucchini
1/4 cup peeled, diced parsnips
1 can (1 pound) unsalted peeled tomatoes,
   coarsely chopped, with liquid
3 sprigs parsley
1 tablespoon tomato paste
1 teaspoon white wine vinegar
1 teaspoon sugar
1 small bay leaf
1/2 teaspoon pepper
1/2 teaspoon dried thyme
   Large pinch dried marjoram
1 teaspoon salt (optional)
3/4 cup frozen peas, thawed
1/4 cup chopped parsley leaves
   French bread with reduced-calorie margarine
   (optional)

1. In a large saucepan, heat vegetable broth to simmer. Add corn sections and green beans; simmer 6–8 minutes.

2. Melt margarine in skillet and saute onion 5 minutes. Add onion to broth, along with potatoes, carrots, celery, sweet potatoes, butternut squash, zucchini, parsnips, and canned tomatoes with liquid.

3. Return soup to simmer. Stir in parsley sprigs, tomato paste, vinegar, sugar, bay leaf, pepper, thyme, marjoram, and (optional) salt. Simmer

30 minutes, uncovered, or until all vegetables are tender. Add peas and simmer 3 minutes or until heated through.

4. Divide hot soup among 4 large soup bowls, about 2 cups each, excluding corn sections. Add 2 corn sections to each soup bowl. Sprinkle 1 tablespoon parsley into each bowl. Serve with heated French bread and reduced-calorie margarine if desired.

Nutritional Data

PER SERVING		EXCHANGES	
Calories:	486	Milk:	0.0
% Calories from fat:	10	Vegetable:	7.0
Fat (gm):	6	Fruit:	0.0
Sat. fat (gm):	0.9	Bread:	4.0
Cholesterol (mg):	0	Meat:	0.0
Sodium (mg):	790	Fat:	0.5
Protein (gm):	14.9		
Carbohydrate (gm):	105		

CREAM OF FAVA BEAN SOUP

This very unusual soup is based on fava beans, which are available canned or dried, in Middle Eastern markets. Although it includes curry powder, the soup is not a "curried" soup as the curry is only one of several flavoring elements. The chives are a necessary flavor ingredient and should not be omitted.

Serves 4

1 can (1 pound) fava beans, rinsed and drained
1 vegetable bouillon cube, low sodium
6 cups water
2 medium onions, coarsely chopped (divided)
1/2 cup coarsely chopped potatoes
2 stalks celery, well peeled, cut in 1-inch lengths
2 tablespoons reduced-calorie margarine
1 large tart, apple, peeled, coarsely chopped
2 teaspoons curry powder
2 teaspoons Worcestershire sauce
1/2 teaspoon pepper
1 1/2 cups fat-free sour cream (divided)
1/2 teaspoon salt (optional)
8 teaspoons chopped fresh chives (divided)
French bread with reduced-calorie margarine (optional)

1. Rinse beans in colander under cold, running tap water.

2. Place bouillon cube and water in large saucepan; heat to boiling and stir to dissolve. Add drained beans, half of chopped onions, potatoes, and celery. Simmer 15–20 minutes or until vegetables are tender.

3. Heat margarine in skillet over medium heat; saute apple and remaining onion 5 minutes. Add curry powder and stir constantly until vegetables are spice-coated. Remove from heat.

4. Scrape skillet contents into saucepan, stirring well. Spoon soup into blender and process until smooth. You may have to do this in 2 batches. Return pureed soup to saucepan.

5. Heat soup to simmer over medium heat. Add Worcestershire sauce, pepper, 1 cup sour cream, and (optional) salt. Whisk to combine and simmer 1 minute.

6. Spoon a generous 1½ cups hot soup into each of 4 large, deep bowls. Garnish each with 2 tablespoons remaining sour cream and 2 teaspoons chives. Serve with heated French bread and reduced-calorie margarine if desired.

Nutritional Data

PER SERVING		EXCHANGES	
Calories:	244	Milk:	0.0
% Calories from fat:	15	Vegetable:	1.0
Fat (gm):	4.3	Fruit:	0.0
Sat. fat (gm):	0.6	Bread:	3.0
Cholesterol (mg):	0	Meat:	0.0
Sodium (mg):	732	Fat:	0.5
Protein (gm):	14.6		
Carbohydrate (gm):	41.7		

SPLIT PEA SOUP WITH 3 ACCOMPANIMENTS

This thick and beautiful green soup is served with cubed sweet potatoes, fresh peas, and croutons.

Serves 4

1 pound split dry green peas
2 vegetable bouillon cubes
6 cups water
1 large square cheesecloth
2 stalks celery, halved
2 sprigs parsley
1 bay leaf
$1/2$ teaspoon dried thyme
2 tablespoons reduced-calorie margarine
$1/2$ cup minced onion
1 cup dry white wine
$1/2$ teaspoon pepper
1 teaspoon salt (optional)
1 cup frozen peas, cooked, drained
1 cup plain croutons, purchased
1 cup peeled, cubed ($1/4$ inch) sweet potatoes, cooked, drained

1. Place dried peas in large pot and add water to cover generously; let soak 4 hours.

2. Place vegetable bouillon and 6 cups water in medium saucepan. Heat to boiling and stir to dissolve bouillon. Turn off heat.

3. Rinse cheesecloth in water and wring out. Lay on counter and place celery halves, parsley sprigs, bay leaf, and thyme in center. Tie up ends tightly to form a package and add to saucepan.

4. Melt margarine in nonstick skillet over medium heat. Saute onion 5 minutes. Add to saucepan. Stir in wine, pepper, and (optional) salt. Add peas.

5. Heat soup to simmer over medium heat. Simmer, uncovered, 30–40 minutes or until peas are soft enough to puree in blender.

6. Discard cheesecloth bag. Spoon peas and liquid into blender container and puree in 2–3 batches. Return puree to soup saucepan.

7. At serving time, place croutons, sweet potatoes, and peas in 3 small serving bowls. Heat soup to simmer, adding as much water as needed. Since soup thickens upon standing, you may need to add 1–2 cups or even more water, depending on consistency.

8. Divide soup among 4 large serving bowls, about 1½ cups each. Pass bowls of sweet potatoes, peas, and croutons and let guests help themselves.

Nutritional Data

PER SERVING		EXCHANGES	
Calories:	561	Milk:	0.0
% Calories from fat:	8	Vegetable:	0.0
Fat (gm):	5.1	Fruit:	0.0
Sat. fat (gm):	0.8	Bread:	6.0
Cholesterol (mg):	0.1	Meat:	2.0
Sodium (mg):	661	Fat:	0.5
Protein (gm):	32.3		
Carbohydrate (gm):	91.1		

POLISH STYLE MUSHROOM-BARLEY-VEGETABLE SOUP

Serves 4

¼ ounce dried mushrooms, imported from Poland, *or* any European variety

9 cups water (divided)

5 vegetable bouillon cubes, low sodium

½ cup medium pearl barley

3 peeled, diced (½ inch) medium baking potatoes

1 cup dry white wine

1 small onion, coarsely chopped

1 stalk celery with leaves, halved

½ cup peeled, quartered baby carrots

2 sprigs parsley

½ teaspoon white pepper

½ teaspoon salt (optional)

    1 cup frozen peas, thawed
   1/2 cup fat-free sour cream (divided)
    4 teaspoons chopped fresh dill (divided)
       French bread with reduced-calorie margarine
       (optional)

1. Place mushrooms in small saucepan. Add 2 cups water, heat to boil, and turn off heat. Let mushrooms soak 1 hour.

2. Place bouillon cubes in large saucepan with remaining 7 cups water. Heat to boiling and stir to dissolve bouillon cubes. Turn off heat.

3. Place barley in separate saucepan; measure 2 cups bouillon from large saucepan and add to barley. Cover and simmer 45–50 minutes or until barley is soft. Check often that liquid has not evaporated. Let barley sit, covered, 5 minutes after cooking.

4. Drain mushrooms, adding mushroom liquid to bouillon. Chop mushrooms coarsely and add to bouillon with potatoes, wine, onion, celery, carrots, parsley, pepper, and (optional) salt. Heat to simmer and cook 20 minutes or until vegetables are soft.

5. Discard celery and parsley. Add barley to soup and simmer 10 minutes. Add peas and simmer 3 minutes.

6. Divide soup among 4 deep soup bowls, about 1 1/2 cups each. Spoon 2 tablespoons sour cream and 1 teaspoon dill into each bowl. Serve with heated French bread and reduced-calorie margarine if desired.

Nutritional Data

PER SERVING		EXCHANGES	
Calories:	293	Milk:	0.0
% Calories from fat:	4	Vegetable:	3.0
Fat (gm):	1.5	Fruit:	0.0
Sat. fat (gm):	0.1	Bread:	3.0
Cholesterol (mg):	0	Meat:	0.0
Sodium (mg):	777	Fat:	0.0
Protein (gm):	9.9		
Carbohydrate (gm):	54.7		

TOMATO SOUP WITH SOUR CREAM AND 4 ACCOMPANIMENTS

Serves 6

5 vegetable bouillon cubes, low-sodium
5 cups water
2 tablespoons reduced-calorie margarine
1 large onion, thinly sliced
1/2 cup peeled, coarsely chopped carrots
1/2 cup peeled, coarsely chopped potatoes
8 large tomatoes, peeled, seeded, quartered
1 cup dry white wine
1 bay leaf
1/2 teaspoon sugar
1/4 teaspoon white pepper
2 pinches dried basil
1/2 teaspoon salt (optional)
1 3/4 cups fat-free sour cream (divided)
6 teaspoons chopped fresh dill
1 1/2 cups peeled, cubed (1/4 inch) baking potatoes,
    cooked, drained (divided)
1 1/2 cups peeled, cubed (1/4 inch) butternut squash,
    or sweet potatoes, cooked, drained (divided)
1 1/2 cups frozen peas, cooked, drained (divided)
1 1/2 cups plain croutons, purchased
1 French bread with reduced-calorie margarine
    (optional)

1. Place bouillon in large saucepan, add water, and heat to boiling. Turn off heat and stir until dissolved.

2. Melt margarine in skillet; saute onion 5 minutes. Spoon onion into soup pan.

3. Add carrots, chopped potatoes, tomatoes, wine, bay leaf, sugar, pepper, basil, and (optional) salt. Simmer 20 minutes or until carrots and potatoes are soft enough to puree in blender.

4. Puree soup in blender; this may have to be done in 2 or 3 batches. Return puree to soup saucepan. Add 1 cup sour cream to soup, stirring with wire whisk to combine.

5. Divide heated soup among 6 large soup bowls, about 1½ cups each. Garnish each bowl with 2 tablespoons remaining sour cream and 1 teaspoon dill.

6. At table, pass bowls of cubed potatoes, squash, peas, and croutons. Guests help themselves. Serve heated French bread and reduced-calorie margarine if desired.

Nutritional Data

PER SERVING		EXCHANGES	
Calories:	302	Milk:	0.0
% Calories from fat:	10	Vegetable:	2.0
Fat (gm):	3.8	Fruit:	0.0
Sat. fat (gm):	0.6	Bread:	3.0
Cholesterol (mg):	0.1	Meat:	2.0
Sodium (mg):	684	Fat:	0.5
Protein (gm):	12.2		
Carbohydrate (gm):	54.3		

ROASTED VEGETABLE MINESTRONE

◆

Oven roasting enhances the natural flavors of vegetables, making this soup a favorite in our repertory. Two cups of cooked macaroni or other-shaped pasta can be substituted for 1 can of the beans.

Serves 8 (about 1³/₄ cups each)

    Olive oil cooking spray
  1 medium eggplant, unpeeled
  1 large Idaho potato, unpeeled
  2 medium zucchini
  2 medium tomatoes
 ½ small butternut squash, peeled
  1 large green bell pepper
  1 large red bell pepper
  1 teaspoon dried rosemary

3/4 teaspoon dried oregano

1/2 teaspoon dried sage

1/4–1/2 teaspoon dried thyme

1 cup coarsely chopped onion

4 cloves garlic, minced

1 can (15 1/2 ounces) cannellini, *or* Great Northern, beans, rinsed, drained

1 can (15 1/2 ounces) red kidney beans, rinsed, drained

7 cups canned vegetable broth

2–3 tablespoons white balsamic vinegar

Salt and pepper, to taste

1. Line large jelly roll pan with aluminum foil and spray with cooking spray. Cut eggplant, potato, zucchini, tomatoes, squash, and bell peppers into 3/4–1-in. pieces. Arrange vegetables on jellyroll pan; spray generously with cooking spray and sprinkle with combined herbs. Bake at 425 degrees until vegetables are browned and tender, 30–40 minutes.

2. Spray large saucepan with cooking spray; heat over medium heat until hot. Saute onion and garlic until tender, about 5 minutes. Add roasted vegetables, beans, and vegetable broth; heat to boiling. Simmer, covered, 10 minutes. Season with vinegar and salt and pepper, to taste.

Nutritional Data

PER SERVING		EXCHANGES	
Calories:	200	Milk:	0.0
% Calories from fat:	5	Vegetable:	3.0
Fat (gm):	1.3	Fruit:	0.0
Sat. fat (gm):	0.1	Bread:	2.0
Cholesterol (mg):	0	Meat:	0.0
Sodium (mg):	292	Fat:	0.0
Protein (gm):	11.6		
Carbohydrate (gm):	45.3		

2
STEWS

Squash and Potato Goulash

Colombian Style Vegetable Stew

Argentinian Stew in a Pumpkin Shell

Hasty Stew

Romanian Stew with Red Wine and Grapes

Russian Style Garden Stroganoff

Garden Vegetable Stew

SQUASH AND POTATO GOULASH

Serves 6

2 cups boiling water
2 vegetable bouillon cubes
2 tablespoons reduced-calorie margarine
1 clove garlic, minced
2 medium onions, coarsely chopped
1½ cups cored, seeded, cubed (¾ inch) red bell pepper
1½ cups cored, seeded, cubed (¾ inch) green bell pepper
3 cups (heaping) peeled, cubed (¾ inch) butternut squash
3 cups (heaping) peeled, cubed (¾ inch) baking potatoes
1 can (16 ounces) peeled tomatoes, coarsely chopped, with liquid
1 cup dry white wine
1 teaspoon salt (optional)
½ teaspoon pepper
3 tablespoons sweet Hungarian paprika (or add a little "hot" Hungarian paprika as desired)
1 cup fat-free sour cream
4½ cups cooked goulash noodles, *or* any wide noodles, hot
¼ cup chopped parsley leaves
   Caraway seeds (optional)

1. Pour boiling water over bouillon cubes in small bowl and reserve. Heat margarine in large saucepan. Saute garlic and onion 5 minutes. Add bell pepper pieces and saute 5 minutes more.

2. Add squash and potato cubes; add tomatoes and liquid. Add bouillon, wine, (optional) salt, and pepper. Simmer 1 hour, uncovered, or until vegetables are tender. Add water as needed.

3. Sprinkle paprika over stew and stir to incorporate. Add sour cream, 2 tablespoons at a time, stirring until well mixed.

4. Spoon noodles onto center of serving plate and spread flat. Spoon goulash onto noodles. Sprinkle with parsley. Pass bowl of caraway seed so guests can sprinkle on goulash if desired.

Nutritional Data

PER SERVING		EXCHANGES	
Calories:	491	Milk:	0.0
% Calories from fat:	9	Vegetable:	3.0
Fat (gm):	5	Fruit:	0.0
Sat. fat (gm):	0.9	Bread:	5.0
Cholesterol (mg):	39.8	Meat:	0.0
Sodium (mg):	533	Fat:	1.0
Protein (gm):	15.3		
Carbohydrate (gm):	95.8		

COLOMBIAN STYLE VEGETABLE STEW

This delicious stew is really a comfort food, meant to be served on a cold night. Be sure to add the cilantro; it's a flavor element, not a garnish.

Serves 6

2 cups boiling water
2 vegetable bouillon cubes
2 tablespoons canola oil
4 garlic cloves, minced
1¼ cups coarsely chopped onion
2 cans (1 pound each) low-sodium peeled tomatoes, coarsely chopped, with liquid
6 small baking potatoes, (5–6 ounces each), peeled, cut in eighths
6 carrots, peeled, cut in 1-inch pieces
6 stalks celery, well peeled, halved lengthwise, cut in 1½-inch lengths
6 ears corn, cut in 1½–2-inch lengths
1 cup dry white wine
2 bay leaves
1½ tablespoons white wine vinegar
1 teaspoon dried cumin

3/4 teaspoon dried oregano
1/2 teaspoon pepper
   Salt (optional)
1 can (about 1 pound) chickpeas, drained
2 cups frozen peas, thawed
3/4 cup chopped cilantro leaves (optional)

1. Pour boiling water over bouillon cubes in small bowl and reserve. Heat oil over medium heat in large saucepan; saute garlic and onion 5 minutes. Add tomatoes with liquid.

2. Add potatoes, carrots, celery, corn, wine, bay leaf, vinegar, cumin, oregano, pepper, (optional) salt, and vegetable bouillon.

3. Heat to boiling, reduce heat to simmer, and cook, uncovered, 45 minutes to 1 hour or until vegetables are tender. Add water if needed during cooking.

4. Place chickpeas in colander under cold running tap water to remove canning liquid; rub them together gently in kitchen towel to remove skins.

5. Add skinless chickpeas and green peas to stew. Simmer 5–10 minutes or until peas are cooked. Divide stew among 6 large dinner plates or deep soup bowls. Sprinkle 2 tablespoons cilantro on each serving if desired.

Nutritional Data

PER SERVING		EXCHANGES	
Calories:	503	Milk:	0.0
% Calories from fat:	14	Vegetable:	4.0
Fat (gm):	8.1	Fruit:	0.0
Sat. fat (gm):	0.8	Bread:	4.5
Cholesterol (mg):	0	Meat:	0.0
Sodium (mg):	757	Fat:	1.5
Protein (gm):	15.8		
Carbohydrate (gm):	93		

ARGENTINIAN STEW IN A PUMPKIN SHELL

We took the meat out of this stew that's traditionally served in a pumpkin shell. Meatless, we think it's much more delicious and beautiful and hope you'll make it year round, whether pumpkins are available or not.

Serves 12

- 4 cups boiling water
- 4 vegetable bouillon cubes
- 3 tablespoons canola oil
- 5 garlic cloves, minced
- 2 cups coarsely chopped red onion
- 1 large green bell pepper, seeded, chopped
- 2 cups dry white wine
- 2 cans (1 pound each) peeled tomatoes, coarsely chopped, with liquid
- 2 tablespoons brown sugar
- 2 tablespoons white wine vinegar
- 2 bay leaves
- 1/2 tablespoon salt
- 1 teaspoon pepper
- 1 teaspoon dried oregano
- 5 cups peeled, cubed (1/2 inch) baking potatoes
- 5 cups peeled, cubed (1/2 inch) sweet potatoes
- 5 cups peeled, cubed (1/2 inch) butternut squash
- 8 ears corn, each cut in 1 1/2–2-inch pieces
- 1 pound zucchini, cut in 3/4-inch slices
- 10 peaches, pitted, halved (or use 20 canned peach halves*)
  Pumpkin Shell (recipe follows)

1. Pour boiling water over bouillon cubes in small bowl and let rest until dissolved. Heat oil in large saucepan over medium heat. Saute garlic and onion 5 minutes. Add green pepper and saute 5 minutes more.

2. Add bouillon broth, white wine, and tomatoes with liquid to pan. Add brown sugar, vinegar, bay leaves, salt, pepper, and oregano. Heat to boiling.

3. Add white potatoes, sweet potatoes and squash; simmer 45 minutes or until vegetables are very tender. Add corn; bury each piece deep in the stew; simmer another 10 minutes until corn is tender.

4. Add zucchini and peach halves* and simmer another 10 minutes or until all ingredients are tender. Add additional water if needed.

5. Serve in Pumpkin Shell (recipe follows) or by itself.

Note: If using canned peach halves, they need only be heated through.

Pumpkin Shell

1 firm pumpkin, 10–12 pounds, round, well-shaped, with no dark spots
1/4 cup reduced-calorie margarine, melted
1/3 cup sugar

1. Preheat oven to 375 degrees. Scrub outside of pumpkin with abrasive cloth under running tap water. Dry well. Draw a 7-inch-diameter chalk circle around stem; cut around circle and lift lid out.

2. Remove fiber and seeds, using spoon to scrape out stubborn bits. Brush inside shell and lid with melted margarine; sprinkle with sugar.

3. Grease a large pie pan. Place pumpkin in pan and set pan in larger roasting pan. Press sheet of aluminum foil over top and sides of pumpkin.

4. Roast pumpkin 30 minutes. Check carefully and continue roasting another 15 minutes, making sure pumpkin does not scorch. Finished pumpkin must be firm enough to hold stew but not hard. Carefully lift pumpkin, in pie pan, out of roasting pan. Turn cooked pumpkin upside down over sink to drain. Replace in pie pan.

5. Spoon hot stew into hot pumpkin shell; return in pie pan to 375-degree oven for 10 minutes more. Bring to table in pie pan, and serve stew with ladle. Use spoon to scoop out some pumpkin to accompany each serving.

Nutritional Data

PER SERVING		EXCHANGES	
Calories:	420	Milk:	0.0
% Calories from fat:	16	Vegetable:	2.0
Fat (gm):	7.5	Fruit:	0.5
Sat. fat (gm):	0.7	Bread:	4.0
Cholesterol (mg):	0	Meat:	0.0
Sodium (mg):	769	Fat:	1.5
Protein (gm):	8		
Carbohydrate (gm):	82		

HASTY STEW

Many vegetable stews are long-simmered to attain their goodness. This stew is easily made in less than 30 minutes and boasts fresh flavors and textures.

Serves 4

Vegetable cooking spray
2 medium onions, cut into wedges
8 ounces mushrooms, sliced
2 cloves garlic, minced
1/4 cup finely chopped parsley leaves
1 teaspoon dried savory leaves
1 bay leaf
2 medium zucchini, sliced
3/4 pound potatoes, unpeeled, cubed
8 ounces cauliflower florets
2 cans (14 1/2 ounces each) vegetable broth
1 large tomato, cut into wedges
Salt, to taste
Pepper, to taste
3 cups cooked millet, *or* couscous, warm

1. Spray large saucepan with vegetable cooking spray; place over medium heat until hot. Saute onions, mushrooms, garlic, and herbs until onions are tender, about 5 minutes.

2. Add vegetables and broth to saucepan; heat to boiling. Reduce heat and simmer, covered, until cauliflower is tender, about 10 minutes. Add tomato during last 5 minutes of cooking time. Season to taste with salt and pepper; discard bay leaf. Serve with millet.

Nutritional Data

PER SERVING		EXCHANGES	
Calories:	404	Milk:	0.0
% Calories from fat:	6	Vegetable:	3.0
Fat (gm):	2.6	Fruit:	0.0
Sat. fat (gm):	0.4	Bread:	4.5
Cholesterol (mg):	0	Meat:	0.0
Sodium (mg):	116	Fat:	0.0
Protein (gm):	13.4		
Carbohydrate (gm):	84.6		

ROMANIAN STEW WITH RED WINE AND GRAPES

Make this Romanian stew, known as ghiveciu, with the same good red wine you serve with it.

Serves 6

4 cups peeled, cubed (3/4 inch) potatoes
4 cups peeled, cubed (3/4 inch) eggplant
2 cups coarsely chopped cauliflower florets
2 1/2 cups coarsely chopped cabbage
2 1/2 cups peeled, cubed (3/4 inch) celery root
1 1/2 cups ends trimmed, 1-inch lengths green beans
1 1/2 cups peeled, halved baby carrots
1/4 cup reduced-calorie margarine (divided)
1 tablespoon finely minced garlic
2 large red onions, coarsely chopped
2 large red bell peppers, cored, seeded, coarsely chopped
Handful parsley leaves, coarsely chopped
1 teaspoon salt
1 teaspoon pepper
3/4 teaspoon dried thyme
1/2 teaspoon dried marjoram
1 cup dry red wine
1/4 cup tomato paste
2 tablespoons molasses
1 bay leaf
2 large tomatoes, peeled, seeded, coarsely chopped
1 cup seedless green grapes
1/2 cup frozen baby peas, thawed

1. Steam vegetables (first 7 ingredients), or cook in 2 inches simmering water until almost tender.

2. Melt 2 tablespoons margarine in nonstick skillet over low heat and saute garlic 1 minute. Raise heat to medium and saute onions and bell peppers 4 minutes. Spoon into medium bowl and add parsley, salt, pepper, thyme, and marjoram. Stir to combine.

3. Preheat oven to 350 degrees. Sprinkle potatoes evenly over bottom of large ovenproof casserole, preferably with large surface area. Sprinkle 1/3 cup bell pepper mixture over potatoes. Arrange eggplant over potatoes and sprinkle another 1/3 cup bell pepper mixture over eggplant.

4. Continue layering vegetables in any order, sprinkling each with 1/3 cup bell pepper mixture. Combine green beans and carrots for top layer, and top casserole with remaining bell pepper mixture.

5. Heat 1 cup water, wine, tomato paste, molasses, bay leaf, and 2 tablespoons margarine to a simmer in small saucepan. Pour over casserole. Cover casserole with foil and bake 45 minutes. Add tomatoes, grapes, and peas to casserole, re-cover, and bake 30 minutes more.

Nutritional Data

PER SERVING		EXCHANGES	
Calories:	339	Milk:	0.0
% Calories from fat:	12	Vegetable:	4.0
Fat (gm):	4.9	Fruit:	0.5
Sat. fat (gm):	0.9	Bread:	2.5
Cholesterol (mg):	0	Meat:	0.0
Sodium (mg):	657	Fat:	1.0
Protein (gm):	8.2		
Carbohydrate (gm):	64.8		

RUSSIAN STYLE GARDEN STROGANOFF

Serves 6

1¹/₃ cups boiling water
2 vegetable bouillon cubes
1 pound baking potatoes, peeled, cut in
   ³/₄-inch cubes
1 pound sweet potatoes, peeled, cut in
   ³/₄-inch cubes
3 tablespoons reduced-calorie margarine
   (divided)
3 medium onions, thinly sliced
¹/₂ pound mushrooms, halved through cap
   and stem
1 cup frozen baby peas
1 tablespoon dry mustard
1 tablespoon sugar
1 tablespoon evaporated skim milk
¹/₂ teaspoon salt
¹/₂ teaspoon pepper
1 cup fat-free sour cream, room temperature
4¹/₂ cups cooked wide noodles
¹/₄ cup coarsely chopped parsley leaves (optional)

1. Combine boiling water with bouillon cubes in a small bowl and reserve.

2. In a large saucepan, cook baking and sweet potatoes in 2 inchs simmering water until tender, 8–10 minutes, and reserve.

3. Melt 1¹/₂ tablespoons margarine over medium heat in large nonstick skillet. Saute onions 5 minutes. Transfer onions to pan with potatoes.

4. Melt remaining 1¹/₂ tablespoons margarine over medium heat in same large skillet. Saute mushrooms 10 minutes. Spoon mushrooms into pan with potatoes, along with reserved bouillon broth.

5. Add peas and simmer 3 minutes. Combine mustard, sugar, milk, salt, and pepper in small bowl and add to stew, stirring gently.

6. Stir in sour cream, a few spoonfuls at a time, mixing well. Heat to simmer. Place noodles on large platter with raised sides and spoon Stroganoff over noodles. Sprinkle with parsley.

Nutritional Data

PER SERVING		EXCHANGES	
Calories:	414	Milk:	0.0
% Calories from fat:	13	Vegetable:	2.0
Fat (gm):	6.1	Fruit:	0.0
Sat. fat (gm):	1	Bread:	4.5
Cholesterol (mg):	39.8	Meat:	0.0
Sodium (mg):	653	Fat:	1.0
Protein (gm):	14.4		
Carbohydrate (gm):	78.9		

GARDEN VEGETABLE STEW

Serves 6

2 tablespoons reduced-calorie margarine
3 cloves garlic, minced
1 large onion, chopped
1½ cups frozen speckled butter beans
3 large potatoes, peeled, cut in 1-inch pieces
2 large tomatoes, peeled, seeded, coarsely
   chopped
½ small cabbage, cored, coarsely chopped
4 medium carrots, peeled, cut in ½-inch pieces
2 turnips, peeled, cut in ½-inch pieces
1 cup trimmed, 1-inch lengths green beans
   Small handful parsley leaves
6 cups water
1 cup dry white wine
2 tablespoons molasses
½ tablespoon salt
2 bay leaves
1 teaspoon dried basil
1 teaspoon dried thyme
½ teaspoon pepper
¾ cup chopped parsley leaves

1. Melt margarine in nonstick skillet over low heat. Saute garlic 1 minute. Add onion and raise heat to medium. Saute 3 minutes. Transfer to large saucepan or stockpot.

2. Add butter beans, potatoes, tomatoes, cabbage, carrots, turnips, green beans, and parsley to stockpot. Add water, wine, molasses, salt, bay leaf, thyme, and pepper.

3. Heat to boiling, reduce heat, and simmer 40 minutes or until most of liquid has evaporated, vegetables are tender, and cabbage has disintegrated. Divide among 6 soup bowls, and sprinkle each serving with 2 tablespoons parsley.

Nutritional Data

PER SERVING		EXCHANGES	
Calories:	248	Milk:	0.0
% Calories from fat:	9	Vegetable:	3.0
Fat (gm):	2.8	Fruit:	0.0
Sat. fat (gm):	0.5	Bread:	2.0
Cholesterol (mg):	0	Meat:	0.0
Sodium (mg):	672	Fat:	0.5
Protein (gm):	8.2		
Carbohydrate (gm):	45.5		

3
PASTA DISHES

"Little Ears" with Artichoke Hearts,
Mushrooms, and Peppers

Pasta with Greens, Raisins, and Pine Nuts

Pasta and 2-Bean Vegetable Soup

Pasta Peperonata

Pasta from Pescia

Southwest Pasta with Cilantro Pesto

Cheese and Vegetable Rotolo with Herb-Tomato Sauce

Cheese-Stuffed Jumbo Shells with Simple Tomato Sauce

Vegetable Lasagna with Eggplant-Tomato Sauce

Pasta Frittata

Tortelloni Primavera

"LITTLE EARS" WITH ARTICHOKE HEARTS, MUSHROOMS, AND PEPPERS

*Because of their shape, orrechiette are often called "little ears."
Other pasta shapes such as cappelletti (little hats), farfalle
(bow ties), or rotini (corkscrews) can be substituted.*

Serves 4

4 ounces shiitake, *or* cremini, mushrooms, sliced
1 red bell pepper, coarsely chopped
1 yellow bell pepper, coarsely chopped
4 cloves garlic, minced
2 teaspoons olive oil, *or* vegetable oil
1/2 can (15-ounce size) artichoke hearts, rinsed, drained, cut into fourths
2 tablespoons minced parsley
Salt, to taste
Pepper, to taste
3 cups (12 ounces) orrechiette ("little ears"), cooked, warm
1/4 cup (1 1/4 ounces) crumbled feta cheese
2 tablespoons coarsely chopped walnuts

1. Saute mushrooms, peppers, and garlic in oil in large skillet until tender, 3–5 minutes. Add artichoke hearts and parsley; cook until hot through, 3–4 minutes. Season to taste with salt and pepper.

2. Spoon vegetable mixture over pasta and toss. Spoon onto plates; sprinkle with feta cheese and walnuts.

Nutritional Data

PER SERVING		EXCHANGES	
Calories:	470	Milk:	0.0
% Calories from fat:	18	Vegetable:	2.0
Fat (gm):	9.7	Fruit:	0.0
Sat. fat (gm):	3.1	Bread:	4.0
Cholesterol (mg):	14.1	Meat:	0.5
Sodium (mg):	233	Fat:	2.0
Protein (gm):	17.1		
Carbohydrate (gm):	80.4		

PASTA WITH GREENS, RAISINS, AND PINE NUTS

Radicchio, escarole, curly endive, kale, or mustard greens can be substituted for the brightly colored oriental kale in this sweet-and-bitter Italian favorite.

Serves 4

1/3 cup dark raisins
1/2 cup warm water
4 medium onions, sliced
4 cloves garlic, minced
1 tablespoon olive oil, *or* vegetable oil
1 teaspoon sugar
12 ounces oriental kale leaves, torn
1/2 cup low-sodium vegetable broth
   Salt, to taste
   Pepper, to taste
12 ounces spaghetti, *or* linguini, cooked, warm
2 tablespoons pine nuts, *or* slivered almonds

1. Soak raisins in warm water 20 minutes; drain and reserve.

2. Saute onions and garlic in oil in large skillet until tender, 3–5 minutes. Stir in sugar; cook over low heat until onions are golden, 10–15 minutes, stirring occasionally.

3. Stir kale and broth into onion mixture; cook, covered, over low heat until kale is wilted, about 10 minutes. Stir in raisins; season to taste with salt and pepper. Spoon mixture over spaghetti and toss; sprinkle with pine nuts.

Nutritional Data

PER SERVING		EXCHANGES	
Calories:	523	Milk:	0.0
% Calories from fat:	14	Vegetable:	3.0
Fat (gm):	8.1	Fruit:	1.0
Sat. fat (gm):	0.8	Bread:	4.5
Cholesterol (mg):	0	Meat:	0.0
Sodium (mg):	67	Fat:	1.5
Protein (gm):	17.6		
Carbohydrate (gm):	97.1		

PASTA AND 2-BEAN VEGETABLE SOUP

Make this soup a day or two in advance so flavors can develop; add the tortelloni when reheating. Any kind of beans, such as Great Northern, garbanzo, pinto, black, etc.,can be used in the soup.

Makes 6 servings (about 1¼ cups each)

Olive oil cooking spray
½ cup sliced leek, *or* green onion, green and white parts
3 cloves garlic, minced
2 tablespoons finely chopped cilantro leaves
2 teaspoons dried basil
2 teaspoons dried oregano
2 cans (14½ ounces each) vegetable broth
1 cup water
1 cup quartered Brussels sprouts
1 cup sliced summer yellow squash
1 cup sliced carrots
1 medium tomato, chopped
1 can (15 ounces) black-eyed peas, rinsed, drained
1 can (15 ounces) dark red kidney beans, rinsed, drained
½ package (9-ounce size) uncooked reduced-fat cheese tortelloni
Salt, to taste
Pepper, to taste

1. Spray large saucepan with cooking spray; heat over medium heat until hot. Saute leek and garlic 1–2 minutes. Stir in herbs and cook until leeks are tender, 3–5 minutes.

2. Add broth, water, vegetables, beans, cheese, and tortelloni; heat to a boil. Reduce heat and simmer, covered, until vegetables are tender and tortelloni are *al dente,* about 10 minutes. Season to taste with salt and pepper.

Nutritional Data

PER SERVING		EXCHANGES	
Calories:	267	Milk:	0.0
% Calories from fat:	14	Vegetable:	2.0
Fat (gm):	4.6	Fruit:	0.0
Sat. fat (gm):	0.8	Bread:	3.0
Cholesterol (mg):	1.3	Meat:	0.0
Sodium (mg):	510	Fat:	0.5
Protein (gm):	14.5		
Carbohydrate (gm):	47.6		

PASTA PEPERONATA

Italian peperonata, a slow-cooked mixture of sweet peppers, onions, and garlic, is also a wonderful filling for pita pockets.

Serves 4

1½ red bell peppers, sliced
1½ green bell peppers, sliced
1½ yellow bell peppers, sliced
3 medium onions, sliced
1 large red onion, sliced
8 cloves garlic, minced
3 tablespoons olive oil, *or* vegetable oil
3 tablespoons water
1 teaspoon sugar
Salt, to taste
Pepper, to taste
12 ounces spaghetti, cooked, warm
¼ cup grated Parmesan cheese (optional)

1. Saute peppers, onions, and garlic in oil in large skillet 2–3 minutes. Add water; cook, covered, over medium to medium-high heat until soft, 2–3 minutes.

2. Stir sugar into peppers mixture; cook uncovered, over medium-low heat until mixture is very soft and browned, about 20 minutes. Season to taste with salt and pepper. Toss with spaghetti; sprinkle with cheese if desired.

Nutritional Data

PER SERVING		EXCHANGES	
Calories:	512	Milk:	0.0
% Calories from fat:	21	Vegetable:	3.0
Fat (gm):	12.1	Fruit:	0.0
Sat. fat (gm):	1.6	Bread:	4.5
Cholesterol (mg):	0	Meat:	0.0
Sodium (mg):	9	Fat:	2.5
Protein (gm):	14.1		
Carbohydrate (gm):	87.6		

PASTA FROM PESCIA

I have fond memories of this hearty dish from the Tuscany region of Italy. Any root vegetable you enjoy can be used in this recipe.

Serve 4

3 cups thinly sliced cabbage
1½ cups halved Brussels sprouts
2 medium carrots, diagonally sliced
2 cloves garlic, minced
½ teaspoon dried sage
⅓ cup low-sodium vegetable broth
8 small new potatoes, unpeeled, cooked
2 tablespoons grated Parmesan cheese
1 tablespoon minced parsley
Salt, to taste
Pepper, to taste
8 ounces rigatoni, *or* ziti, cooked, warm

1. Heat cabbage, Brussels sprouts, carrots, garlic, sage, and vegetable broth to boiling in large skillet. Reduce heat and simmer, covered, until cabbage is wilted, about 5 minutes. Add potatoes and cook, uncovered, until liquid is gone and cabbage is lightly browned, about 5 minutes.

2. Stir cheese and parsley into vegetables; season to taste with salt and pepper. Spoon mixture over pasta and toss.

Nutritional Data

PER SERVING		EXCHANGES	
Calories:	486	Milk:	0.0
% Calories from fat:	5	Vegetable:	3.0
Fat (gm):	2.5	Fruit:	0.0
Sat. fat (gm):	0.9	Bread:	6.0
Cholesterol (mg):	2.5	Meat:	0.0
Sodium (mg):	144	Fat:	0.0
Protein (gm):	16.9		
Carbohydrate (gm):	102.3		

SOUTHWEST PASTA WITH CILANTRO PESTO

If poblano peppers are not available, substitute green bell peppers and add 1/2 to 1 teaspoon finely chopped jalapeño pepper to the onions when sauteing. Dried cilantro is not an acceptable substitute for the fresh; if not available, substitute fresh basil or oregano.

Serves 4

- 2 medium zucchini, sliced
- 2 cups peeled, cubed acorn squash
- 1 medium onion, sliced
- 2 poblano peppers, sliced
- 1 teaspoon dried oregano
- 1/4 teaspoon dried cumin
- 1 tablespoon olive oil, *or* vegetable oil
- 1/2 cup low-sodium vegetable broth
- 2 medium tomatoes, cut into wedges
  Salt, to taste
  Pepper, to taste
- 12 ounces yolk-free fettuccine, *or* other flat pasta, cooked, warm
  Cilantro Pesto (recipe follows)

1. Saute squash, onion, poblano peppers, oregano, and cumin in oil in large skillet 3 minutes; add broth and heat to boiling. Reduce heat and simmer, covered, until acorn squash is crisp-tender, about 5 minutes. Add tomato wedges; cook, covered, until tomatoes soften, 3–4 minutes. Season to taste with salt and pepper.

2. Toss fettuccine with Cilantro Pesto; spoon onto serving platter and top with vegetable mixture.

Cilantro Pesto

Makes about ½ cup

- ¾ cup (packed) fresh cilantro leaves
- ¼ cup (packed) fresh parsley leaves
- 2 tablespoons grated Parmesan cheese
- 2 tablespoons pine nuts, *or* slivered almonds
- 1 clove garlic, minced
- ¼ teaspoon finely chopped jalapeño pepper
- 1 tablespoon olive oil, *or* vegetable oil
- 1½ teaspoons lemon juice
  - Salt, to taste
  - Pepper, to taste

1. Process cilantro, parsley, cheese, nuts, garlic, jalapeño pepper, oil, and lemon juice in food processor or blender until smooth; season to taste with salt and pepper.

2. Refrigerate until serving time; serve at room temperature.

Nutritional Data

PER SERVING		EXCHANGES	
Calories:	502	Milk:	0.0
% Calories from fat:	23	Vegetable:	2.0
Fat (gm):	13.4	Fruit:	0.0
Sat. fat (gm):	1.9	Bread:	4.5
Cholesterol (mg):	2.5	Meat:	0.0
Sodium (mg):	132	Fat:	2.5
Protein (gm):	18.2		
Carbohydrate (gm):	82.1		

CHEESE AND VEGETABLE ROTOLO WITH HERB-TOMATO SAUCE

Serve the rotolo whole, or cut each into thirds, arranging the slices cut sides up on the tomato sauce.

Serves 4

- ½ cup chopped onion
- ½ cup chopped carrot
- ½ cup chopped mushrooms
- 2 cloves garlic, minced
- 1 teaspoon dried basil
- 1 teaspoon olive oil, *or* vegetable oil
- 2 cups small broccoli florets, cooked until crisp-tender
- ¾ cups fat-free ricotta cheese
- ½ package (8-ounce size) fat-free cream cheese (not tub type), softened
- ¼ cup grated Parmesan cheese
- ½ cup (2 ounces) shredded reduced-fat mozzarella cheese
- ½ teaspoon salt
- ½ teaspoon pepper
- 8 lasagna noodles (8 ounces), cooked *al dente*
  Herb-Tomato Sauce (recipe follows)
  Parsley sprigs, as garnish

1. Saute onion, carrot, mushrooms, garlic, and basil in oil in large skillet until tender; stir in broccoli.

2. Process sauteed vegetables, cheeses, salt, and pepper in food processor, using pulse technique, until cheeses are mixed and vegetables are finely chopped.

3. Spread about ⅓ cup vegetable-cheese mixture on 1 lasagna noodle; roll up and place, seam side down, in lightly greased 13 x 9-inch baking pan. Repeat with remaining noodles and vegetable-cheese mixture. Bake at 350 degrees, loosely covered with aluminum foil, until hot, 30 to 40 minutes.

4. Serve rotolo whole or, if desired, cut each rotolo into 3 pieces. Spoon about 1/3 cup Herb-Tomato Sauce on each plate; arrange rotolo on sauce. Garnish with parsley.

Herb-Tomato Sauce

Makes about 2²/₃ cups

1 cup chopped red bell pepper
1/4 cup chopped onion
1 clove garlic, minced
1 teaspoon dried oregano
1 teaspoon dried basil
1 tablespoon olive oil, *or* vegetable oil
2 large tomatoes, chopped
3/4 cup reduced-sodium vegetable broth

1. Saute pepper, onion, garlic, and herbs in oil in medium skillet until tender, about 5 minutes. Add tomatoes; saute 3 minutes. Add broth and heat to boil. Reduce heat and simmer, uncovered, until thickened to sauce consistency, about 10 minutes, stirring occasionally.

Nutritional Data

PER SERVING		EXCHANGES	
Calories:	361	Milk:	0.5
% Calories from fat:	27	Vegetable:	2.5
Fat (gm):	11.3	Fruit:	0.0
Sat. fat (gm):	3.4	Bread:	1.5
Cholesterol (mg):	20.1	Meat:	2.0
Sodium (mg):	808	Fat:	1.0
Protein (gm):	26		
Carbohydrate (gm):	42.8		

CHEESE-STUFFED JUMBO SHELLS WITH SIMPLE TOMATO SAUCE

This dish can be made a day or two in advance of serving. Simply stuff the shells and refrigerate, covered. Spoon sauce over shells when ready to heat.

Serves 6

- 1 package (15 ounces) part-skim ricotta cheese
- 1 cup grated Parmesan cheese (divided)
- 2 eggs
- 1/2 cup finely chopped parsley leaves (divided)
- 2 cloves garlic, minced
- 1/2 teaspoon salt
- 1/4 teaspoon pepper
- 24 jumbo pasta shells, cooked

1. Mix ricotta, 3/4 cup Parmesan cheese, eggs, 1/4 cup parsley, garlic, salt, and pepper. Stuff shells with mixture and arrange in baking pan. Spoon Simple Tomato Sauce over shells.

2. Bake, covered, until hot through, 20–30 minutes. Sprinkle with combined remaining 1/4 cup Parmesan cheese and 1/4 cup parsley before serving.

Simple Tomato Sauce

Makes about 3 cups

- 1 small onion, finely chopped
- 1 clove garlic, minced
- 1 tablespoon canola, *or* olive, oil
- 2 cans (14 1/2 ounces each) low-sodium tomatoes, undrained, coarsely chopped
- 1/2 teaspoon sugar
- 1/2 teaspoon dried basil
- 1/4 teaspoon dried oregano
- 1 bay leaf
- 1/2 teaspoon salt
- 1/4 teaspoon pepper

1. Saute onion and garlic in oil in large skillet 2–3 minutes. Add tomatoes and remaining ingredients; heat to boiling. Reduce heat and simmer, covered, 20 minutes. Discard bay leaf.

2. Process tomato mixture in food processor or blender until coarsely pureed. Serve hot.

Nutritional Data

PER SERVING		EXCHANGES	
Calories:	430	Milk:	0.0
% Calories from fat:	21	Vegetable:	2.0
Fat (gm):	10.4	Fruit:	0.0
Sat. fat (gm):	4.1	Bread:	3.0
Cholesterol (mg):	84.2	Meat:	2.5
Sodium (mg):	749	Fat:	0.5
Protein (gm):	28.3		
Carbohydrate (gm):	58.5		

VEGETABLE LASAGNA WITH EGGPLANT-TOMATO SAUCE

Any fresh vegetables in season can be used in this versatile, garden-fresh lasagna. Assemble up to a day in advance and refrigerate until ready to bake.

Serves 12

Vegetable cooking spray
2 cups thinly sliced mushrooms
1 cup thinly sliced carrots
1 medium zucchini, sliced
2 cups chopped tomatoes
2 cups spinach leaves
1 teaspoon dried oregano
3 cups fat-free ricotta cheese
1/2 cup grated Parmesan cheese
Eggplant-Tomato Sauce (recipe follows)
12 lasagna noodles (12 ounces), cooked *al dente*
1 cup (4 ounces) shredded reduced-fat Monterey Jack, *or* mozzarella, cheese

1. Spray large skillet with cooking spray; heat over medium heat until hot. Saute mushrooms, carrots, and zucchini until crisp-tender, 5–10 minutes. Stir in tomatoes, spinach, and oregano; cook, covered, until tomatoes are soft and spinach is wilted, 3–5 minutes.

2. Mix ricotta and Parmesan cheeses.

3. Spread 1 cup Eggplant-Tomato Sauce over bottom of 13 x 9 inch baking pan; top with 4 lasagna noodles. Spoon 1/3 of vegetable mixture over noodles; spoon 1/3 of cheese mixture over vegetables; top with 1 cup Eggplant-Tomato Sauce. Repeat layers 2 times, ending with Eggplant-Tomato Sauce. Sprinkle with Monterey Jack cheese evenly over top.

4. Bake at 350 degrees, covered with aluminum foil, until hot, 45–60 minutes. Cool 5–10 minutes before cutting.

Eggplant-Tomato Sauce

Makes about 4 cups

- 1 medium eggplant (3/4 pound), unpeeled, cubed (1 inch)
- 1 cup chopped onion
- 8 cloves garlic, minced
- 1 tablespoon olive-oil, *or* vegetable oil
- 4 cups chopped tomatoes
- 3/4 teaspoon dried oregano
- 3/4 teaspoon dried thyme
- 1–2 teaspoons sugar (optional)
- 1/2 teaspoon salt
- 1/2 teaspoon pepper

1. Saute eggplant, onion, and garlic in oil in large skillet for 5 minutes; add tomatoes, herbs, and sugar. Cook, covered, until vegetables are tender, 10–15 minutes. Cook, uncovered, until excess liquid is gone, about 5 minutes. Stir in salt and pepper.

Nutritional Data

PER SERVING		EXCHANGES	
Calories:	205	Milk:	0.5
% Calories from fat:	23	Vegetable:	2.0
Fat (gm):	5.6	Fruit:	0.0
Sat. fat (gm):	2	Bread:	0.5
Cholesterol (mg):	16.1	Meat:	1.5
Sodium (mg):	299	Fat:	0.0
Protein (gm):	17		
Carbohydrate (gm):	25.9		

PASTA FRITTATA

A pasta frittata is a delicious way to use leftover linguine, fettuccine, or spaghetti. Vary the vegetables in the topping according to season and availability.

Serves 4

- 2 medium carrots, sliced
- 8 ounces cauliflower florets
- 1 cup sliced red bell peppers
- 1/3 cup sliced green onion, green and white parts
- 2 cloves garlic, minced
- 1 tablespoon olive oil, *or* vegetable oil
- 1 medium zucchini, sliced
- 1 medium tomato, chopped
- 1 teaspoon dried basil
- 3/4 teaspoon dried oregano
- 3/4 teaspoon dried marjoram
- 4 ounces thin spaghetti, cooked
- 4 egg whites
- 2 tablespoons grated Parmesan cheese
- 1/2 teaspoon salt
- 1/4 teaspoon pepper
  Olive oil cooking spray
  Minced parsley, as garnish

1. Saute carrots, cauliflower, bell pepper, onion, and garlic in oil in medium skillet until carrots are crisp-tender, 5–7 minutes. Stir in zucchini, tomato, and herbs; saute until vegetables are tender, about 5 minutes more.

2. In bowl, mix spaghetti, egg whites, cheese, salt, and pepper. Spray medium skillet with cooking spray. Add pasta mixture, spreading it evenly. Cook, uncovered, over medium to medium-low heat until browned on bottom, about 5 minutes. Turn and cook until browned on other side, about 5 minutes. Slide frittata onto serving platter; spoon vegetable mixture over and sprinkle with parsley.

Nutritional Data

PER SERVING		EXCHANGES	
Calories:	249	Milk:	0.0
% Calories from fat:	19	Vegetable:	3.0
Fat (gm):	5.4	Fruit:	0.0
Sat. fat (gm):	1.2	Bread:	2.0
Cholesterol (mg):	2.5	Meat:	0.0
Sodium (mg):	416	Fat:	0.5
Protein (gm):	12		
Carbohydrate (gm):	39.5		

TORTELLONI PRIMAVERA

A sprinkling of balsamic vinegar adds a creative flavor twist to this colorful primavera.

Serves 6

     4 sun-dried tomato halves (not packed in oil)
   1/2 cup boiling water
     2 cups cut asparagus (1 1/2-inch pieces)
     2 medium summer yellow squash, sliced
     1 teaspoon dried basil
   1/2 teaspoon dried tarragon
     1 cup halved cherry tomatoes
     4 ounces trimmed snow peas
     1 package (9 ounces) reduced-fat tortelloni,
        cooked, warm
     3 tablespoons grated Parmesan cheese
        White balsamic vinegar (optional)

1. Soak sun-dried tomatoes in water until soft, 10–15 minutes. Drain and reserve liquid; slice tomatoes.

2. Heat asparagus, squash, basil, tarragon, and reserved tomato liquid to boiling in large skillet. Reduce heat and cook, covered, 3 minutes. Add dried tomatoes, cherry tomatoes, and snow peas; simmer, covered, 5 minutes or until snow peas are tender.

3. Toss tortelloni with vegetables. Spoon tortelloni mixture onto plates; sprinkle with cheese and a few drops of vinegar.

Nutritional Data

PER SERVING		EXCHANGES	
Calories:	167	Milk:	0.0
% Calories from fat:	12	Vegetable:	1.0
Fat (gm):	2.3	Fruit:	0.0
Sat. fat (gm):	1.2	Bread:	1.5
Cholesterol (mg):	5	Meat:	0.5
Sodium (mg):	270	Fat:	0.0
Protein (gm):	9.7		
Carbohydrate (gm):	28.2		

4
RICE AND
GRAIN DISHES

Vegetarian Fried Rice

Barley with Peppers and Potatoes

Barley-Vegetable Chowder

All-Season Risotto

Risotto-Vegetable Cakes

Kasha with Green Pasta and Vegetables

Curried Couscous

Black Eyes and Greens with Millet

Millet with Artichoke Hearts and Vegetables

Wheat Berry and Lentil Stew with Dumplings

Mushroom and Asparagus Pilaf

Wheat Berries Waldorf

VEGETARIAN FRIED RICE

The combination of wild and white rice adds a new dimension to an Asian favorite. Lightly scrambled egg is a traditional addition to many fried rice recipes; it can be omitted, if desired.

Serves 4 (about 1½ cups each)

Vegetable cooking spray
2 cups sliced broccoli florets and stalks
2 ounces ends trimmed, diagonally sliced snow peas
2 medium carrots, sliced
¾ cup chopped celery
¾ cup bean sprouts
¾ cup sliced shiitake, *or* white, mushrooms
½ cup chopped red or green bell pepper
1 clove garlic, minced
1 teaspoon finely chopped ginger root
½ cup vegetable broth
2 tablespoons reduced-sodium soy sauce
1½ cups cooked white rice
1½ cups cooked wild rice
1 egg, lightly scrambled, crumbled

1. Spray wok or large skillet with cooking spray; heat over medium heat until hot. Stir-fry vegetables and ginger root until crisp-tender, 5–8 minutes.

2. Add broth and soy sauce to wok; stir in rice and scrambled egg and cook 2–3 minutes more.

Nutritional Data

PER SERVING		EXCHANGES	
Calories:	236	Milk:	0.0
% Calories from fat:	8	Vegetable:	2.5
Fat (gm):	2.1	Fruit:	0.0
Sat. fat (gm):	0.5	Bread:	2.5
Cholesterol (mg):	53.3	Meat:	0.0
Sodium (mg):	472	Fat:	0.0
Protein (gm):	10.4		
Carbohydrate (gm):	46.6		

BARLEY WITH PEPPERS AND POTATOES

◆

*Here's a variation on the delicious Mexican rajas con papas.
If poblano peppers are not available, substitute green bell
peppers and 1–2 teaspoons of minced jalapeños.*

Serves 4 (about 1¹/₂ cups each)

6   large poblano peppers, sliced
2   medium onions, chopped
1   tablespoon olive oil, *or* vegetable oil
2¹/₂ pounds russet potatoes, unpeeled, cooked, cubed
2   cups cooked barley
2   tablespoons finely chopped cilantro leaves
1   teaspoon dried cumin
    Salt, to taste
    Cayenne, to taste

1. Saute peppers and onions in oil in large skillet until crisp-tender, about 5 minutes. Add potatoes; saute until browned, 5–8 minutes.

2. Add barley to skillet; cook over medium heat until hot through, 3–4 minutes. Stir in cilantro and cumin. Season to taste with salt and pepper.

Nutritional Data

PER SERVING		EXCHANGES	
Calories:	464	Milk:	0.0
% Calories from fat:	8	Vegetable:	4.0
Fat (gm):	4.4	Fruit:	0.0
Sat. fat (gm):	0.6	Bread:	5.0
Cholesterol (mg):	0	Meat:	0.0
Sodium (mg):	29.3	Fat:	0.0
Protein (gm):	10.2		
Carbohydrate (gm):	99.7		

BARLEY-VEGETABLE CHOWDER

◆

A perfect soup for crisp autumn days;
substitute any desired vegetables.

Serves 4 (about 1³/₄ cups each)

2 cans (14½ ounces each) vegetable broth
²/₃ cup barley
   Vegetable cooking spray
2 small onions, chopped
1 leek, sliced
2 cloves garlic, minced
1 cup fresh, *or* frozen, lima beans
1 cup fresh, *or* frozen, whole-kernel corn
1 cup finely chopped cabbage
2 medium carrots, sliced
1 teaspoon dried savory
½ teaspoon dried thyme
1 bay leaf
2 tablespoons flour
½ cup skim milk

1. Heat ½ can of vegetable broth to boiling in small saucepan; stir in barley and let stand 15–30 minutes.

2. Spray large saucepan with cooking spray; heat over medium heat until hot. Saute onions, leek, and garlic until tender, about 5 minutes. Add remaining vegetables and herbs; saute 2–3 minutes. Add remaining 1½ cans broth and broth and barley mixture; heat to boil. Reduce heat and simmer, covered, until barley is tender, about 20 minutes.

3. Heat soup to boiling. Mix flour and milk and stir into soup. Boil, stirring constantly, until thickened. Discard bay leaf.

Nutritional Data

PER SERVING		EXCHANGES	
Calories:	312	Milk:	0.0
% Calories from fat:	3	Vegetable:	2.5
Fat (gm):	1	Fruit:	0.0
Sat. fat (gm):	0.2	Bread:	3.5
Cholesterol (mg):	0.5	Meat:	0.0
Sodium (mg):	150	Fat:	0.0
Protein (gm):	11.1		
Carbohydrate (gm):	68.2		

ALL-SEASON RISOTTO

A blending of summer and winter squash provides color and flavor to this creamy risotto dish. If preferred, the reserved vegetable mixture can be heated and served to the side rather than mixing it into the risotto.

Serves 6 (about 1¹/₃ cups each)

- 2 cups peeled, cubed winter yellow squash (acorn, butternut, Hubbard, etc.)
- 1 medium zucchini, sliced
- 1¹/₂ cups sliced cremini, *or* white, mushrooms
- 1 medium red bell pepper, chopped
- 6 plum tomatoes, cut into fourths
- 2 teaspoons dried oregano
- 2 tablespoons olive oil, *or* vegetable oil (divided)
- 1 cup chopped onion
- 2 cloves garlic, minced
- 1¹/₂ cups arborio rice
- 2 cans (14¹/₂ ounces each) reduced-sodium vegetable broth
- 2 cups water
- ¹/₄ cup grated Parmesan cheese
- 1 can (15¹/₂ ounces) black beans, rinsed, drained
- ¹/₂ cup frozen peas, thawed
- Salt, to taste
- Pepper, to taste
- Parmesan cheese, grated (optional)

1. Saute squash, mushrooms, bell pepper, tomatoes, and oregano in 1 tablespoon oil in large skillet until tender; remove from heat and reserve.

2. Heat remaining 1 tablespoon oil until hot in large saucepan; add onion and garlic and saute until tender, 3–4 minutes. Add rice; cook 2–3 minutes, stirring occasionally.

3. Heat vegetable broth and water to simmering in medium saucepan; reduce heat to low and keep warm. Add broth to rice mixture, ¹/₂ cup at a time, stirring constantly until broth is absorbed before adding next ¹/₂ cup. Continue process until rice is *al dente* and mixture is creamy, 20–25 minutes.

4. Stir cheese, beans, and peas into rice mixture. Stir in reserved vegetables and heat until hot. Season to taste with salt and pepper. Serve with additional grated cheese if desired.

Nutritional Data

PER SERVING		EXCHANGES	
Calories:	383	Milk:	0.0
% Calories from fat:	18	Vegetable:	2.0
Fat (gm):	8.2	Fruit:	0.0
Sat. fat (gm):	1.6	Bread:	4.0
Cholesterol (mg):	3.3	Meat:	0.0
Sodium (mg):	557	Fat:	1.0
Protein (gm):	17.4		
Carbohydrate (gm):	68.3		

RISOTTO-VEGETABLE CAKES

A great way to use leftover risotto!

Serves 4

Olive oil cooking spray
1 medium onion, finely chopped
2 cloves garlic, minced
2 teaspoons dried oregano (divided)
1 cup arborio rice
3 cups vegetable broth
1 cup water
1/4 cup shredded reduced-fat Cheddar, *or* Monterey Jack, cheese
2 tablespoons grated Parmesan cheese (divided)
1 medium zucchini, chopped
2 medium carrots, chopped
1 medium red bell pepper, chopped
1/2 cup chopped celery
2 egg whites
2/3 cup Italian-seasoned breadcrumbs
8 beefsteak tomatoes, thickly (1/2 inch) sliced
Salt, to taste
Pepper, to taste

1. Spray medium saucepan with cooking spray; heat over medium heat until hot. Saute onion, garlic, and 1 teaspoon oregano until tender, about 3 minutes. Add rice; cook 2–3 minutes.

2. Heat vegetable broth and water to simmering in medium saucepan; reduce heat to low to keep warm. Add broth to rice mixture, ½ cup at a time, stirring constantly until broth is absorbed before adding next ½ cup. Continue process until rice is *al dente* and mixture is creamy, 20–25 minutes. Stir in Cheddar cheese and 1 tablespoon Parmesan cheese. Cool to room temperature.

3. Spray large skillet with cooking spray; heat over medium heat until hot. Saute zucchini, carrots, bell pepper, and celery until tender, 5–8 minutes. Stir vegetables, egg whites, and breadcrumbs into rice mixture.

4. Form rice mixture into 8 patties, each a scant ¾ in. thick. Broil on lightly greased broiler pan, 6 inches from heat source, until browned, 2–4 minutes each side. Top each patty with tomato slice; sprinkle with remaining 1 teaspoon oregano, remaining 1 tablespoon Parmesan cheese, salt, and pepper. Broil again until browned on top, 2–3 minutes.

Nutritional Data

PER SERVING		EXCHANGES	
Calories:	400	Milk:	0.0
% Calories from fat:	7	Vegetable:	3.0
Fat (gm):	2.9	Fruit:	0.0
Sat. fat (gm):	1.3	Bread:	4.0
Cholesterol (mg):	6.3	Meat:	0.5
Sodium (mg):	805	Fat:	0.0
Protein (gm):	13.9		
Carbohydrate (gm):	77.1		

KASHA WITH GREEN PASTA AND VEGETABLES

Kasha, or buckwheat groats, is usually available in supermarkets and often in health food stores, but it is not well known. Classified as a grain, it has a delicious taste and a satisfying texture.

Serves 6

6 tablespoons reduced-calorie margarine, (divided)
1½ cups coarse (whole granulation) kasha
1 egg, beaten
3 vegetable bouillon cubes
4 cups boiling water
1¼ cups small dried spinach pasta, such as shells, bows, or rotini, cooked
½ cup finely chopped green onion and tops
1 cup frozen peas, thawed
1 cup broccoli florets, cooked
6 tablespoons finely chopped parsley leaves

1. Melt 1 tablespoon margarine in large skillet; stir in kasha. Add egg and cook over low heat, stirring constantly, until egg disappears.

2. Dissolve bouillon cubes in boiling water; add to kasha mixture and heat to boiling. Reduce heat and simmer, covered, until kasha is tender and liquid is absorbed, 25–30 minutes; stir in pasta.

3. Saute green onions in remaining 5 tablespoons margarine in small skillet until tender, about 5 minutes. Stir green onions, peas, and broccoli into kasha mixture; cook over medium heat until hot through, 3–4 minutes. Spoon into serving bowl and sprinkle with parsley.

Nutritional Data

PER SERVING		EXCHANGES	
Calories:	269	Milk:	0.0
% Calories from fat:	27	Vegetable:	0.0
Fat (gm):	8.6	Fruit:	0.0
Sat. fat (gm):	1.6	Bread:	3.0
Cholesterol (mg):	43	Meat:	0.0
Sodium (mg):	648	Fat:	1.0
Protein (gm):	9.8		
Carbohydrate (gm):	42.8		

CURRIED COUSCOUS

Couscous, a staple in Mediterranean countries, is one of the fastest, easiest grains to cook. Serve with a selection of condiments so that the dish can be enjoyed with a variety of flavor accents.

Serve 4 (about 1½ cups each)

Vegetable cooking spray
8 ounces fresh, *or* frozen (thawed), whole okra
1 medium onion, chopped
2 cloves garlic, chopped
2 tablespoons finely chopped parsley
1 cup frozen whole-kernel corn
1 cup sliced mushrooms
2 medium carrots, sliced
1½ teaspoons curry powder
1 cup vegetable broth
⅔ cup couscous, packaged
1 medium tomato, chopped
Salt, to taste
Pepper, to taste
Cucumber Yogurt (recipe follows)
Onion-Chutney Relish (recipe follows)
¼ cup chopped unsalted peanuts
¼ cup dark raisins

1. Spray large saucepan with cooking spray; heat over medium heat until hot. Saute okra, onion, garlic, and parsley until onion is tender, about 5 minutes. Stir in corn, mushrooms, carrots, and curry powder; cook 2 minutes.

2. Add broth to saucepan and heat to boil; reduce heat and simmer, covered, until vegetables are tender, 8–10 minutes. Stir in couscous and tomatoes. Remove from heat and let stand, covered, until couscous is tender and broth absorbed, about 5 minutes. Season to taste with salt and pepper.

3. Spoon couscous mixture into serving bowl; serve with Cucumber Yogurt, Onion-Chutney Relish, peanuts, and raisins.

Cucumber Yogurt

Makes about 1 cup

2/3 cup fat-free plain yogurt
2/3 cup seeded, finely chopped cucumber
1 teaspoon dried dill weed

1. Combine all ingredients; refrigerate until ready to serve.

Onion-Chutney Relish

Makes about 1 cup

Vegetable cooking spray
4 medium onions, chopped
1/2 cup chopped mango chutney, purchased
1–1 1/2 teaspoons dried mint leaves

1. Spray large skillet with cooking spray; heat over medium heat until hot. Saute onion 3–5 minutes; reduce heat to low and cook until they are very soft and golden, about 15 minutes.

2. Mix onion, chutney, and mint; refrigerate until ready to serve.

Nutritional Data

PER SERVING		EXCHANGES	
Calories:	449	Milk:	0.0
% Calories from fat:	11	Vegetable:	4.0
Fat (gm):	5.6	Fruit:	2.0
Sat. fat (gm):	0.8	Bread:	2.5
Cholesterol (mg):	0.7	Meat:	0.0
Sodium (mg):	90	Fat:	1.0
Protein (gm):	14.2		
Carbohydrate (gm):	90.4		

BLACK EYES AND GREENS WITH MILLET

A new twist to Hopping John! Your preference in greens might also be kale or mustard greens.

Serves 4 (about 1½ cups each)

Vegetable cooking spray
1 medium onion, sliced
2 cloves garlic, minced
1 can (14½ ounces) vegetable broth
3 tablespoons red wine vinegar
6 cups coarsely chopped turnip greens
2 large tomatoes, cut in wedges
1 can (15 ounces) black-eyed peas, drained
1 cup millet
2 tablespoons finely chopped cilantro leaves
  Salt, to taste
  Pepper, to taste
  Red pepper sauce, to taste

1. Spray large saucepan with cooking spray; heat over medium heat until hot. Saute onion and garlic until tender, about 5 minutes. Add broth and vinegar; heat to boil. Add greens and tomatoes to saucepan; reduce heat and simmer, covered, until greens are wilted, about 5 minutes.

2. Stir black-eyed peas and millet into saucepan; simmer, covered, until all liquid is absorbed, about 20 minutes. Remove from heat and let stand 5–10 minutes. Stir in cilantro; season to taste with salt and pepper. Serve with red pepper sauce if desired.

Nutritional Data

PER SERVING		EXCHANGES	
Calories:	360	Milk:	0.0
% Calories from fat:	18	Vegetable:	2.0
Fat (gm):	7.3	Fruit:	0.0
Sat. fat (gm):	1.1	Bread:	3.5
Cholesterol (mg):	0	Meat:	0.0
Sodium (mg):	374	Fat:	1.5
Protein (gm):	12		
Carbohydrate (gm):	62.4		

MILLET WITH ARTICHOKE HEARTS AND VEGETABLES

*Deeply browned artichoke hearts, seasoned with garlic,
add robust flavor to this grain and vegetable combination.*

Makes 4 servings (about 1¹/₂ cups each)

- ¹/₂ cup millet
- 1³/₄ cups vegetable broth (divided)
- 2 cans (15 ounces each) artichoke hearts, drained, cut in halves
- 1 tablespoon margarine
- ¹/₄ teaspoon garlic powder
- 2 medium onions, chopped
- 1 medium green bell pepper, chopped
- 2 cloves garlic, minced
- 2 medium tomatoes, chopped
- 1 medium eggplant, unpeeled, cut in 1-inch pieces
- 1 medium zucchini, sliced
- 1 bay leaf
- 2 tablespoons finely chopped parsley leaves
  Salt, to taste
  Pepper, to taste

1. Cook millet in large skillet over medium heat until toasted, 2–3 minutes. Add 1¹/₄ cups broth and heat to boiling; reduce heat and simmer, covered, until millet is tender and broth is absorbed, about 15 minutes. Remove from heat and let stand, covered, 10 minutes.

2. Saute artichoke hearts in margarine in large skillet until well browned on all sides, 5–7 minutes. Remove from skillet and sprinkle with garlic powder.

3. Add onions, green pepper, and garlic to skillet used in Step 2. Saute until tender, 3–5 minutes. Add remaining ¹/₂ cup broth, remaining vegetables, bay leaf, and parsley; heat to boiling. Reduce heat and simmer, covered, until eggplant is tender, 15–20 minutes.

4. Add millet and artichoke hearts to skillet; cook until hot through, 3–4 minutes. Discard bay leaf and season to taste with salt and pepper.

Nutritional Data

PER SERVING		EXCHANGES	
Calories:	320	Milk:	0.0
% Calories from fat:	13	Vegetable:	7.0
Fat (gm):	5.3	Fruit:	0.0
Sat. fat (gm):	0.9	Bread:	1.5
Cholesterol (mg):	0	Meat:	0.0
Sodium (mg):	286	Fat:	1.0
Protein (gm):	13.4		
Carbohydrate (gm):	63.6		

WHEAT BERRY AND LENTIL STEW WITH DUMPLINGS

Wheat berries have a wonderful, chewy nutty texture.
They can be readily purchased at health food stores;
barley or another preferred grain, can be substituted.

Serves 6 (about 1½ cups each)

1 cup wheat berries
Vegetable cooking spray
2 medium onions, chopped
½ cup chopped celery
4 cloves garlic, minced
1 teaspoon dried savory
3 cups vegetable broth
2 pounds russet potatoes, unpeeled, cubed
2 medium carrots, sliced
1½ cups lentils
Herb Dumplings (recipe follows)

1. Cover wheat berries with 2–3 inches water in saucepan; let stand overnight. Heat to boiling; reduce heat and simmer, covered, until wheat berries are tender, 45–55 minutes. Drain.

2. Spray large saucepan with cooking spray; heat over medium heat until hot. Saute onions, celery, garlic, and savory until onions are tender, 3–5 minutes. Add broth, potatoes, carrots, and lentils and heat to boil; reduce heat and simmer, covered, until vegetables are just tender, 10–15 minutes. Stir in wheat berries.

3. Spoon Herb Dumplings mixture onto top of stew; cook, uncovered, 5 minutes. Cook, covered, until dumplings are dry, 5–10 minutes longer.

Herb Dumplings

$1/2$ cup all-purpose flour
$1/2$ cup yellow cornmeal
$1^1/2$ teaspoons baking powder
$1/2$ teaspoon dried sage
$1/4$ teaspoon dried thyme
$1/2$ teaspoon salt
2 tablespoons vegetable shortening
$1/2$ cup skim milk

1. Combine flour, cornmeal, baking powder, sage, thyme, and salt in medium bowl. Cut in shortening with pastry blender or 2 knives until mixture resembles coarse crumbs. Stir in milk.

Nutritional Data

PER SERVING		EXCHANGES	
Calories:	467	Milk:	0.0
% Calories from fat:	10	Vegetable:	2.0
Fat (gm):	5.5	Fruit:	0.0
Sat. fat (gm):	1.3	Bread:	5.0
Cholesterol (mg):	0.3	Meat:	0.0
Sodium (mg):	347	Fat:	1.0
Protein (gm):	14.5		
Carbohydrate (gm):	92		

MUSHROOM AND ASPARAGUS PILAF

The dried Chinese black or shiitake mushrooms impart a hearty, woodsy flavor to this pilaf. The mushrooms are available in large supermarkets or oriental groceries.

Serves 6 (about 1½ cups each)

3⅓ cups vegetable broth (divided)
2 cups dried Chinese mushrooms
Vegetable cooking spray
2 large onions, chopped
4 cloves garlic, minced
2 teaspoons dried basil
½ teaspoon dried thyme
½ teaspoon dried savory
1½ pounds asparagus, cut in 1½-inch pieces
¼ cup dry sherry, *or* vegetable broth
2 packages (6 ounces each) wheat pilaf
¼ teaspoon Tabasco, *or* red pepper, sauce
Salt, to taste
Pepper, to taste
4 green onions, green and white parts, thinly sliced
¼ cup toasted pecan halves

1. Heat 2 cups vegetable broth to boiling; pour over mushrooms in bowl and let stand until mushrooms are softened, 10–15 minutes. Drain, reserving broth. Slice mushrooms, discarding tough stems.

2. Spray large skillet with cooking spray; heat over medium heat until hot. Saute mushrooms, onions, garlic, and herbs until onions are tender, about 5 minutes. Add asparagus; saute 5 minutes more.

3. Add sherry, reserved vegetable broth from mushrooms, and remaining 1⅓ cups vegetable broth to skillet; heat to boiling. Stir in wheat pilaf (discard spice packet). Reduce heat and simmer, covered, until broth is absorbed and pilaf is tender, 3–5 minutes. Stir in Tabasco sauce; season to taste with salt and pepper. Spoon into serving bowl; sprinkle with green onions and pecans.

Nutritional Data

PER SERVING		EXCHANGES	
Calories:	436	Milk:	0.0
% Calories from fat:	22	Vegetable:	2.0
Fat (gm):	11.6	Fruit:	0.0
Sat. fat (gm):	0.9	Bread:	4.0
Cholesterol (mg):	0	Meat:	0.0
Sodium (mg):	636	Fat:	2.0
Protein (gm):	15.5		
Carbohydrate (gm):	72.6		

WHEAT BERRIES WALDORF

*Wheat berries have a wonderful "toothsome" texture.
They can be purchased at health food stores. If wheat
berries are unavailable, substitute 2/3 cup bulgur;
soak bulgur in 1 1/3 cups water until tender.*

Serves 4 (about 1 1/2 cups each)

1 1/4 cups wheat berries
1 1/2 cups peeled, cored, cubed pineapple
2 medium oranges, cut in segments
1 large apple, cored, cubed
1 cup thinly sliced fennel bulb
3 tablespoons coarsely chopped walnuts
2 tablespoons finely chopped parsley leaves
1/3 cup fat-free mayonnaise
2 1/2 teaspoons Dijon-style mustard
1 1/2 tablespoons lemon juice
2 teaspoons sugar
3/4 teaspoon crushed fennel seeds
Lettuce leaves, as garnish

1. Cover wheat berries with 2–3 inches water in saucepan; let stand overnight. Heat to boiling; reduce heat and simmer, covered, until wheat berries are tender, 45–55 minutes. Drain and cool.

2. Combine wheat berries, fruit, fennel, walnuts, and parsley in bowl. In separate bowl, combine remaining ingredients, except lettuce; spoon over salad and toss. Serve on lettuce-lined plates.

Nutritional Data

PER SERVING		EXCHANGES	
Calories:	319	Milk:	0.0
% Calories from fat:	12	Vegetable:	0.0
Fat (gm):	4.6	Fruit:	1.5
Sat. fat (gm):	0.3	Bread:	3.0
Cholesterol (mg):	0	Meat:	0.0
Sodium (mg):	310	Fat:	0.5
Protein (gm):	7.8		
Carbohydrate (gm):	65.8		

5
BEAN DISHES

Louisiana Style Red Beans and Rice

Puerto Rican Style Red Beans and Rice

East Indian Black Beans with Rice

Boston Baked Beans and Brown Bread

Black and White Bean Chili

Vegetarian Cassoulet

Chuckwagon Beans

Deep-Dish Tamale Pie

Beans and Fruit au Gratin

LOUISIANA STYLE RED BEANS AND RICE

Serves 4

1½ cups small dried red beans*
  3 tablespoons reduced-calorie margarine
  3 cloves garlic, minced
⅓ cup minced red onion
1¼ cups minced green onion, green and white
    parts (divided)
¼ cup minced celery leaves
¼ teaspoon dried sage
¼ teaspoon dried thyme
¾ teaspoon light salt
¼ teaspoon cayenne
  3 cups cooked long-grain white rice, hot

1. Place beans in saucepan with ample water to cover. Let soak 6 to 8 hours or overnight, taking care that beans are always covered with water.

2. Drain beans. Place in saucepan with fresh water to cover. Simmer, uncovered, 40 minutes or until tender. Drain, reserving water, and measure out 3 cups beans.

3. Melt margarine in large saucepan over low heat. Add garlic and saute 1 minute. Raise heat to medium and add red onion, 6 tablespoons scallions, and celery leaves. Saute 4 minutes.

4. Add sage, thyme, salt, and cayenne. Stir over heat for a few seconds. Add beans and ¾ cup reserved bean water. Simmer 10 minutes, stirring often with wooden spoon.

5. Arrange rice in a flat circle on serving platter. Spoon bean mixture over rice, leaving a white rice border. Sprinkle 6 tablespoons of remaining scallions over beans. Place remaining scallions in serving bowl and pass with rice and beans.

Note: If small red beans are not available, dried red kidney beans can be substituted, but they will need several hours of simmering before they soften.

Nutritional Data

PER SERVING		EXCHANGES	
Calories:	381	Milk:	0.0
% Calories from fat:	12	Vegetable:	1.0
Fat (gm):	5.3	Fruit:	0.0
Sat. fat (gm):	0.9	Bread:	4.0
Cholesterol (mg):	0	Meat:	0.5
Sodium (mg):	305	Fat:	1.0
Protein (gm):	17.5		
Carbohydrate (gm):	67		

PUERTO RICAN STYLE RED BEANS AND RICE

In this dish, the raw rice is added to the dish and simmered in the beans' soaking liquid until done. But we use canned beans for convenience and cook our rice separately because it guarantees success and, we feel, improves the dish. A taste for the musky-flavored achiote seeds must sometimes be acquired, so we have made them optional. If you've never tried them, be prepared for an unusual, albeit flavorful, experience.

Serves 4

- 2 cans (15–16 ounces each) red pinto beans, drained
- 2 tablespoons canola oil
- 1½ tablespoons achiote seeds* (optional)
- ¾ cup coarsely chopped onion
- ¾ teaspoon minced fresh garlic
- ¾ cup coarsely chopped green bell pepper
- 1 large tomato, peeled, seeded, coarsely chopped
- 6 tablespoons chopped cilantro leaves (divided)
- ½ teaspoon dried oregano
- ½ teaspoon pepper
  Salt, to taste
- 1 cup long-grain white rice, cooked
- ¼ cup water

1. Empty cans of beans into colander, rinse with cold water, and drain. Reserve beans.

2. Heat oil in small saucepan with achiote seeds. Saute 10 minutes over low heat. Strain oil and discard seeds.

3. Place 2 tablespoons strained oil in large saucepan over medium heat. Add onion and garlic; saute 5 minutes. Add green pepper and saute 5 minutes. Add tomato, 2 tablespoons cilantro, oregano, pepper, and (optional) salt as desired. Simmer 10 minutes over low heat, stirring often so mixture does not burn. It should be quite dry after simmering.

4. Stir rice and beans into saucepan with 1/4 cup water. Heat, stirring frequently, until very hot. Spoon into serving bowl, and garnish with remaining 1/4 cup cilantro. Serve immediately.

*Note: Achiote seeds, the rusty-colored seeds of the annatto tree, are available in Latin American markets and some general supermarkets.

Nutritional Data

PER SERVING		EXCHANGES	
Calories:	477	Milk:	0.0
% Calories from fat:	17	Vegetable:	2.0
Fat (gm):	9.3	Fruit:	0.0
Sat. fat (gm):	0.6	Bread:	5.0
Cholesterol (mg):	0	Meat:	0.0
Sodium (mg):	784	Fat:	1.5
Protein (gm):	20		
Carbohydrate (gm):	85.3		

EAST INDIAN BLACK BEANS WITH RICE

This delicious, fast-and-easy-to-make dish is enlivened with Indian spices, but it's not a curry and it doesn't have the traditional curry taste.

Serves 4

- 2 tablespoons reduced-calorie margarine
- 3/4 cup minced onion
- 1½ -inch piece fresh ginger, peeled, minced
- 1½ teaspoons dried coriander plus 1 pinch (divided)
- 1/2 teaspoon salt
- 3/4 teaspoon dried cumin plus 1 pinch (divided)
- 1/2 teaspoon dried turmeric
- 1/4 teaspoon dried red pepper plus 1 pinch (divided)
- 3 cups canned black beans, well washed, drained
- 1/2 cup water
  Big pinch dried cinnamon
  Big pinch dried cardamom
  Big pinch dried cloves
- 3 cups cooked rice, hot
- 1/4 cup minced fresh coriander leaves

1. Heat margarine over medium heat in nonstick skillet. Add onion and ginger, and saute 4–5 minutes or until onions are soft.

2. Add 1½ teaspoons coriander, salt, 3/4 teaspoon cumin, turmeric, and 1/4 teaspoon red pepper to skillet and cook 1 minute, stirring constantly with wooden spoon.

3. Spoon skillet contents into large saucepan. Add beans and 1/2 cup water and heat to boil. Sprinkle remaining pinch of coriander, cumin, and red pepper over beans. Add pinches of cinnamon, cardamom, and cloves and stir to combine.

4. Spoon rice onto serving plate and spoon bean mixture over rice, leaving a white border. Sprinkle coriander over beans and rice and serve immediately.

Nutritional Data

PER SERVING		EXCHANGES	
Calories:	299	Milk:	0.0
% Calories from fat:	12	Vegetable:	0.0
Fat (gm):	4.5	Fruit:	0.0
Sat. fat (gm):	0.6	Bread:	4.0
Cholesterol (mg):	0	Meat:	0.0
Sodium (mg):	734	Fat:	0.5
Protein (gm):	14.1		
Carbohydrate (gm):	58.6		

BOSTON BAKED BEANS AND BROWN BREAD

This well-known combination turns out to be complementary on a nutritional level as well as a gastronomic level. Eaten together, the bread and beans provide the 10 amino acids necessary to form whole protein. Incidentally, our homemade version of this specialty is far superior to those that are commercially available.

Serves 4

Boston Baked Beans

1½ cups dried pea beans
¼ cup molasses
3 tablespoons brown sugar
¾ teaspoon dry mustard
⅓ teaspoon salt
¼ teaspoon pepper
2 cups water
½ medium onion

1. Place beans in large pot with ample water to cover and allow to soak overnight. Next day, drain colander under cold running tap water. Pick over beans and discard any discolored ones.

2. Preheat oven to 300 degrees. Measure out 3 cups beans and place in bean pot with cover or casserole with cover.

3. Add molasses, brown sugar, dry mustard, salt, and pepper to beans plus 2 cups water. Stir well to combine. Bury onion half in bean mixture.

4. Bake 6–10 hours or until tender. Check beans every hour to see if they need liquid. Each time they appear dry, add another cup of water. You will need to add several cups of water during baking.

5. Serve immediately, or allow to cool. Store covered in refrigerator. Reheat beans before serving if desired. Serve with Boston Brown Bread.

Boston Brown Bread

$1/2$ cup raisins
Vegetable cooking spray
$1/2$ cup graham flour
$1/2$ cup rye flour
$1/2$ cup yellow cornmeal
$1/2$ teaspoon baking soda
$1/4$ teaspoon salt
$1/3$ cup dark molasses
1 cup buttermilk
Reduced-calorie margarine (optional)

1. In a large pot with cover, place a raised rack, platform, or steamer rack. Prepare raisins by placing them in baking pan in a single layer and freezing until raisins are stiff. Spray a 14- or 15-ounce coffee can on bottom and sides with vegetable cooking spray.

2. Sift graham flour, rye flour, cornmeal, baking soda, and salt together. Place in medium bowl. Add molasses and buttermilk, stir to combine.

3. Place frozen raisins in blender container and chop. Stir raisins into batter.

4. Spoon batter into prepared can. Place a small piece of foil over top of can and secure with rubberband.

5. Add enough hot tap water to pot to reach bottom of rack. Turn burner to high. When water boils, reduce heat to medium. Set can on rack in pot, and cover.

6. Bread should steam $2^1/4$–$2^1/2$ hours. Check pot often during steaming, and add water as needed to keep it level with rack.

7. When bread is done, remove foil. If serving bread immediately, invert can onto serving platter. It may be necessary to loosen bread from sides of can with long knife. Bring to table with Boston Baked Beans. Pass reduced-calorie margarine if desired.

Note: If serving bread at a later time, allow it to cool in can with foil in place. Refrigerate until serving. At serving time, return can to pot and steam as before until heated, 10–15 minutes.

Nutritional Data

PER SERVING		EXCHANGES	
Calories:	536	Milk:	0.0
% Calories from fat:	4	Vegetable:	0.0
Fat (gm):	2.6	Fruit:	1.0
Sat. fat (gm):	0.6	Bread:	6.5
Cholesterol (mg):	2.3	Meat:	0.0
Sodium (mg):	622	Fat:	0.0
Protein (gm):	18.5		
Carbohydrate (gm):	114.4		

BLACK AND WHITE BEAN CHILI

Serves 4

1½ cups canned white beans, such as
   Great Northern
1½ cups canned black beans
1½ tablespoons canola oil
 1 teaspoon finely minced garlic
 1 cup minced red onion
 1 cup minced red bell pepper
 4 teaspoons chili powder
 ½ teaspoon salt (optional)
 ½ teaspoon (scant) dried cumin
 ⅛ teaspoon dried oregano
   Large pinch cayenne
 3 cans (14½ ounces each) low-sodium peeled
   tomatoes with liquid
 6 tablespoons plus 4 teaspoons chopped cilantro
   leaves (divided)
 8 teaspoons fat-free sour cream
 8 teaspoons reduced-calorie Cheddar cheese

1. Place black and white beans in colander under cold running tap water to remove canning liquid. Drain and reserve.

2. Heat oil over medium-low heat in nonstick skillet. Add garlic, red onion, and red bell pepper. Saute 5 minutes, stirring often with wooden spoon.

3. Sprinkle chili powder, (optional) salt, cumin, oregano, and cayenne over vegetables, and stir for a few seconds until spices are incorporated.

4. Quarter canned tomatoes and place in large saucepan with tomato liquid and beans. Use spatula to scrape skillet contents into saucepan. Cover and simmer 10 minutes. Stir in 1/4 cup cilantro leaves.

5. Divide chili among four large soup bowls. Top each bowl with 2 teaspoons sour cream and 2 teaspoons cheese. Sprinkle remaining cilantro over all.

Nutritional Data

PER SERVING		EXCHANGES	
Calories:	363	Milk:	0.0
% Calories from fat:	19	Vegetable:	4.0
Fat (gm):	8.5	Fruit:	0.0
Sat. fat (gm):	1	Bread:	3.0
Cholesterol (mg):	2.8	Meat:	0.0
Sodium (mg):	834	Fat:	1.0
Protein (gm):	21.3		
Carbohydrate (gm):	61.9		

VEGETARIAN CASSOULET

◆

This cassoulet contains none of the meat or animal products of the famous French dish but is nonetheless very good. We suggest serving it with a grain such as couscous to form complementary whole protein.

Serves 4

1 1/2 cups dried white kidney beans
2 tablespoons reduced-calorie margarine
3 cloves garlic, minced
3/4 cup finely chopped onion
3 large tomatoes, peeled, seeded, chopped
1 cup white wine (divided)
1/2 cup plus 2 tablespoons water
1 cup parsley leaves (divided)
1 bay leaf
1 1/8 teaspoons salt (divided)
1/2 teaspoon plus 1/8 teaspoon dried thyme (divided)

$\frac{1}{4}$ teaspoon black pepper
Large pinch dried basil
1 tablespoon molasses
2 teaspoons tomato paste
2 slices reduced-calorie white bread
$\frac{1}{4}$ teaspoon mild paprika
Pinch white pepper
3 cups cooked couscous, hot (optional)
$\frac{1}{4}$ cup chopped parsley, *or* cilantro, leaves

1. Soak beans overnight in water to cover. Drain and place in large saucepan with water to cover. Heat to boil. Simmer $1\frac{1}{2}$ hours or until very tender, adding water as needed. Drain and reserve.

2. Preheat oven to 400 degrees. Melt margarine in nonstick skillet over low heat. Saute garlic 1 minute. Add onions and raise heat to medium. Saute garlic and onions 3–4 minutes. Add tomatoes and $\frac{1}{2}$ cup wine. Simmer 20 minutes or until pan liquid evaporates.

3. Measure out 3 cups beans and spoon into bowl. Add onion-tomato mixture, remaining $\frac{1}{2}$ cup wine, $\frac{1}{2}$ cup water, 1 cup parsley leaves, bay leaf, 1 teaspoon salt, $\frac{1}{2}$ teaspoon thyme, black pepper, and basil. Mix molasses and tomato paste with 2 tablespoons water and stir into beans. Spoon bean mixture into a shallow casserole with large surface area.

4. Toast bread lightly so it dries but does not color. Process in food processor with remaining cup of parsley leaves. Stir in remaining $\frac{1}{8}$ teaspoon salt, $\frac{1}{8}$ teaspoon thyme, paprika, and white pepper. Puree until fine breadcrumbs result.

5. Sprinkle crumb mixture on top of casserole. Bake 30–45 minutes or until crust is golden brown . Remove bay leaf before serving.

6. At serving time, if desired, ladle $\frac{3}{4}$ cup couscous onto each serving plate, and top with serving of cassoulet. Sprinkle each serving with 1 tablespoon chopped parsley or cilantro.

Nutritional Data

PER SERVING		EXCHANGES	
Calories:	315	Milk:	0.0
% Calories from fat:	12	Vegetable:	2.0
Fat (gm):	4.4	Fruit:	0.0
Sat. fat (gm):	0.8	Bread:	3.0
Cholesterol (mg):	0	Meat:	0.5
Sodium (mg):	772	Fat:	0.5
Protein (gm):	14.7		
Carbohydrate (gm):	48.7		

CHUCKWAGON BEANS

Although it isn't traditional, brown rice forms a complementary whole protein with these beans and is delicious as well.

Serves 4

1½ cups dried pinto beans, *or* red kidney beans
2 medium tomatoes, peeled, seeded, chopped
2 large onions, coarsely chopped
⅔ cup brown sugar, lightly packed
¼ cup molasses
⅓ cup coarsely chopped celery leaves
⅓ cup coarsely chopped parsley leaves
3 large garlic cloves
1 cup water
1¼ teaspoons salt
2 teaspoons dry mustard
1½ teaspoons crushed red pepper flakes
½ teaspoon dried coriander
⅛ teaspoon ground nutmeg
⅛ teaspoon dried cinnamon
   Large pinch ground cloves
1 bay leaf, halved
3 cups cooked brown rice, hot (optional)

1. Soak beans overnight in ample water to cover. Next day, rinse in colander under cold running tap water. Discard discolored beans.

2. Preheat oven to 300 degrees. Measure out 3 cups beans and place in earthenware casserole with cover or ceramic casserole with cover. Add tomatoes, onions, brown sugar, and molasses and stir to combine.

3. Place celery, parsley, and garlic in blender container with 1 cup water and process until pureed. Mix into beans.

4. Sprinkle salt, mustard, pepper flakes, coriander, nutmeg, cinnamon, and cloves over beans. Add bay leaf and 1 cup water. Stir to combine.

5. Cover beans and place in oven. Bake 6–10 hours or until beans are tender. Check beans every hour and add cup of water each time they look dry. You will need to add several cups during baking. Serve with hot brown rice, if desired.

Nutritional Data

PER SERVING		EXCHANGES	
Calories:	416	Milk:	0.0
% Calories from fat:	3	Vegetable:	2.0
Fat (gm):	1.6	Fruit:	0.0
Sat. fat (gm):	0.2	Bread:	5.0
Cholesterol (mg):	0	Meat:	0.0
Sodium (mg):	714	Fat:	0.0
Protein (gm):	12.7		
Carbohydrate (gm):	91.5		

DEEP-DISH TAMALE PIE

Serves 4

Filling

Vegetable cooking spray
1 cup small dried red beans, *or* 2 cups canned pink or red beans (do not use kidney beans)
6 sun-dried tomatoes
1 tablespoon reduced-calorie margarine
²/₃ cup minced red onion
³/₄ cup cubed (¹/₂ inch) green bell pepper
1¹/₂ cups halved frozen ears baby corn, thawed
1 tablespoon (scant) chili powder
¹/₂ teaspoon salt (optional)
³/₄ teaspoon dried cumin
¹/₄ teaspoon cayenne
1 cup peeled, seeded, coarsely chopped fresh tomato
³/₄ cup water
¹/₄ cup grated reduced-calorie Cheddar cheese

Cornmeal Topping

³/₄ cup yellow cornmeal
1 tablespoon flour
4 teaspoons sugar
1¹/₄ teaspoons baking powder
¹/₄ teaspoon salt
¹/₄ teaspoon baking soda

⅓ cup buttermilk

1 egg, beaten

1 tablespoon reduced-calorie margarine, melted

1. Make filling: Soak dried beans overnight in water to cover. Drain, place in saucepan, cover with water, and simmer 2–3 hours or until tender. If using canned beans, place in colander and rinse under cold running tap water. Soak dried tomatoes in boiling water 15 minutes.

2. Preheat oven to 400 degrees. Heat margarine in large nonstick skillet over medium heat. Saute onion, green pepper, and corn 3 minutes. Drain and chop dried tomatoes and add to skillet with chili powder, (optional) salt, cumin, and cayenne. Cook 30 seconds, stirring to combine.

3. Stir in beans, fresh tomato, and ¾ cup water. Simmer 5 minutes. Mixture should contain enough liquid for a stew; if it does not, add a few additional tablespoons water.

4. Spoon mixture into 8-cup ovenproof casserole, preferably with large surface area (8 x 12-inch oval baking dish is ideal). Sprinkle cheese over top.

5. Make cornmeal topping: Sift cornmeal, flour, sugar, baking powder, salt, and baking soda together into bowl. Mix buttermilk, egg, and margarine together, and stir into dry ingredients.

6. Spread topping over casserole mixture. Bake 25 minutes or until topping is golden brown.

Nutritional Data

PER SERVING		EXCHANGES	
Calories:	459	Milk:	0.0
% Calories from fat:	15	Vegetable:	2.0
Fat (gm):	8.4	Fruit:	0.0
Sat. fat (gm):	2.3	Bread:	4.5
Cholesterol (mg):	61.6	Meat:	0.5
Sodium (mg):	675	Fat:	1.0
Protein (gm):	22.1		
Carbohydrate (gm):	81.4		

BEANS AND FRUIT AU GRATIN

---◆---

This German-style combination of fruit, beans, and vegetables sounds unusual but is really delicious.

Serves 4

1 cup peeled, sliced (1/3 inch) carrots
1 cup 1-inch pieces green beans
1 cup canned navy, or Great Northern, beans, drained
1 cup peeled, sliced (1/3 inch) potatoes
2 cups peeled, sliced (1/3 inch) green apples, preferably Granny Smiths
1 cup peeled, sliced (1/3 inch) pears
1/2 teaspoon (scant) dried rosemary plus 2 pinches (divided)
2 teaspoons sugar
1/2 teaspoon salt (divided)
1/8 teaspoon plus 2 pinches white pepper (divided)
2 slices reduced-calorie white bread, made into crumbs in blender or food processor
2 pinches hot paprika
2 tablespoons reduced-calorie margarine (divided)

1. Preheat oven to 350 degrees. Cook carrots and green beans in water to cover until almost tender; drain in colander. Place canned beans in colander under cold running water to remove canning liquid.

2. Combine carrots, green beans, canned beans, potatoes, apples, and pears in 8-cup ovenproof casserole with cover.

3. Crumble rosemary with fingertips. Combine 1/2 teaspoon rosemary with sugar, 1/4 teaspoon salt, and 1/8 teaspoon white pepper. Add to vegetable and fruit mixture, and toss lightly to combine. Cover and bake 30 minutes.

4. Make au gratin topping: Combine breadcrumbs, remaining 1/4 teaspoon salt, remaining 2 pinches rosemary, 2 pinches white pepper, and paprika. Work 2 teaspoons margarine into crumb mixture with fingertips until well combined.

5. When casserole is done, remove from oven and raise heat to 400 degrees. Dot casserole with remaining 4 teaspoons margarine and toss lightly to combine.

6. Sprinkle topping over casserole. Return to oven 15 minutes or until crumbs are lightly browned. Serve immediately.

Nutritional Data

PER SERVING		EXCHANGES	
Calories:	294	Milk:	0.0
% Calories from fat:	12	Vegetable:	1.5
Fat (gm):	4.2	Fruit:	1.0
Sat. fat (gm):	0.7	Bread:	2.5
Cholesterol (mg):	0	Meat:	0.0
Sodium (mg):	758	Fat:	0.5
Protein (gm):	8.5		
Carbohydrate (gm):	60.4		

6
ROASTED AND GRILLED DISHES

Grilled Vegetable Fajitas

Oriental Satay

Roasted Potato Salad

Root Veggies and Mashed Potatoes

Roasted Squash, Moroccan Style

Grill-Roasted Vegetables with Polenta

Veggie Pocket Sandwiches

GRILLED VEGETABLE FAJITAS

Cactus leaves and poblano peppers are commonly available today in large supermarkets as well as Mexican groceries. If unavailable, substitute another vegetable, such as zucchini, for the cactus and green bell peppers and one jalapeño chili for the poblano peppers.

Serves 4 (2 fajitas each)

4 medium poblano peppers, cut in 1-inch slices
3 large tomatoes, cut in wedges
2 medium onions, cut in wedges
4 large cactus paddles *(nopales)*, cut in 1-inch slices
  Vegetable cooking spray
2 tablespoons olive oil, *or* vegetable oil
2 tablespoons white distilled vinegar
1 tablespoon lime juice
2 cloves garlic, minced
3–4 dashes cayenne
8 flour, *or* corn, tortillas, warm
1/4 cup finely chopped cilantro
8 tablespoons fat-free sour cream
4 avocado slices

1. Spray vegetables with cooking spray; place on grill over medium-hot coals. Grill, turning occasionally, until vegetables are browned and tender, about 30 minutes (or bake on greased aluminum-foil-lined jellyroll pan at 400 degrees until brown and tender, 30–40 minutes). Combine vegetables in bowl.

2. Mix oil, vinegar, lime juice, garlic, and pepper; drizzle over vegetables and toss. Spoon about 1/2 cup of dressed vegetable mixture on each tortilla. Sprinkle with cilantro, top with 1 tablespoon sour cream, and roll up.

3. Place fajitas and avocado slices on serving plates.

Nutritional Data

PER SERVING		EXCHANGES	
Calories:	414	Milk:	0.0
% Calories from fat:	29	Vegetable:	3.0
Fat (gm):	14.1	Fruit:	0.0
Sat. fat (gm):	2.3	Bread:	3.5
Cholesterol (mg):	0	Meat:	0.0
Sodium (mg):	47	Fat:	2.0
Protein (gm):	12.6		
Carbohydrate (gm):	64.2		

ORIENTAL SATAY

*Vegetables are roasted with a Fragrant Basting Sauce
and served with a chunky Peanut Sauce.*

Serves 4

½ medium acorn squash, peeled, seeded, cut in
   1-inch pieces
1 pound broccoli florets
½ pound fresh or frozen (thawed) whole okra
2 medium summer yellow squash, cut in
   1-inch slices
8 ounces pearl onions, peeled
   Fragrant Basting Sauce (recipe follows)
3 cups cooked rice, warm
   Peanut Sauce (recipe follows)

1. Cook acorn squash in 2 inches simmering water in medium saucepan
   until beginning to soften, about 2 minutes; drain.

2. Arrange vegetables on skewers and place on lightly greased aluminum-
   foil-lined jellyroll pan. Bake on top rack of oven at 550 degrees/broil
   until lightly browned, about 5 minutes. Baste with half the Basting
   Sauce, and bake 1–2 minutes longer. Turn vegetables and repeat for
   other side, using remainder of Basting Sauce.

3. Arrange skewers on plates; serve with rice and Peanut Sauce.

Fragrant Basting Sauce

Makes about 3/4 cup

2 tablespoons reduced-sodium soy sauce
¼ cup rice wine, *or* dry sherry

$^1/_4$ cup (packed) light brown sugar
1 tablespoon finely chopped green onion, green
and white parts
1 teaspoon grated lemon rind
2 teaspoons sesame oil
1 teaspoon black bean sauce
1–2 dashes hot chili sesame oil

1. Combine all ingredients.

Peanut Sauce

Makes about $^2/_3$ cup

3 tablespoons reduced-sodium soy sauce
3 tablespoons chunky peanut butter
2$^1/_2$ tablespoons sugar
$^1/_4$ cup thinly sliced green onion, green and white
parts
1 tablespoon grated ginger root

1. Combine all ingredients.

Nutritional Data

PER SERVING		EXCHANGES	
Calories:	452	Milk:	0.0
% Calories from fat:	20	Vegetable:	3.0
Fat (gm):	10.3	Fruit:	0.0
Sat. fat (gm):	1.8	Bread:	4.0
Cholesterol (mg):	0	Meat:	0.0
Sodium (mg):	775	Fat:	2.0
Protein (gm):	13.4		
Carbohydrate (gm):	78.9		

ROASTED POTATO SALAD

---

*The potatoes are roasted until crusty and brown,
lending a unique flavor to this salad.*

Serves 4 (about 1½ cups each)

Olive oil cooking spray
8 cups cut up (each in eighths) small, unpeeled Idaho potatoes
Salt, to taste
Pepper, to taste
1 medium onion, chopped
1 medium red bell pepper, chopped
1 medium green bell pepper, chopped
½ cup frozen peas, thawed
½ cup thinly sliced celery
Dilled Mayonnaise Dressing (recipe follows)
Lettuce, as garnish
4 rye rolls

1. Spray aluminum-foil-lined jellyroll pan with cooking spray. Arrange potatoes on pan in single layer; spray generously with cooking spray and sprinkle lightly with salt and pepper. Bake at 400 degrees until potatoes are browned, crusty, and tender, about 30 minutes. Cool to room temperature.

2. Combine potatoes, onion, peppers, peas, and celery in large bowl; spoon Dilled Mayonnaise Dressing over and toss. Serve in lettuce-lined bowls with rye rolls.

Dilled Mayonnaise Dressing

Makes about ¾ cup

¼ cup fat-free mayonnaise, *or* salad dressing
¼ cup fat-free plain yogurt
2 tablespoons Dijon-style mustard
1 tablespoon lemon juice
2 cloves garlic, minced
½ teaspoon dried dill weed

1. Mix all ingredients; refrigerate until serving time.

Nutritional Data

PER SERVING		EXCHANGES	
Calories:	492	Milk:	0.0
% Calories from fat:	4	Vegetable:	1.0
Fat (gm):	2	Fruit:	0.0
Sat. fat (gm):	0.4	Bread:	6.5
Cholesterol (mg):	0.3	Meat:	0.0
Sodium (mg):	611	Fat:	0.0
Protein (gm):	13.3		
Carbohydrate (gm):	107.7		

ROOT VEGGIES AND MASHED POTATOES

A selection of winter root vegetables, roasted to perfection and served with garlic-spiked mashed potatoes.

Serves 4 (about 1½ cups each)

Vegetable cooking spray
3 medium beets, peeled, sliced
3 medium turnips, peeled, sliced
3 medium carrots, diagonally cut in 1-inch pieces
1 leek (white parts only), cut in 1-inch pieces
2½ cups halved Brussels sprouts
1 tablespoon caraway seeds
Salt, to taste
Pepper, to taste
1½ pounds Idaho potatoes, unpeeled, cubed
4 cloves garlic, peeled
¼ cup skim milk, hot
2 tablespoons margarine, cut in pieces

1. Spray aluminum-foil-lined jellyroll pan with cooking spray. Arrange beets, turnips, carrots, leek, and Brussels sprouts on pan in single layer; spray generously with cooking spray. Sprinkle vegetables with caraway seeds; sprinkle lightly with salt and pepper. Bake at 400 degrees until vegetables are tender and lightly browned, about 40 minutes.

2. Cook potatoes and garlic in 2-inches simmering water in covered saucepan until tender, 10–15 minutes; drain. Mash potatoes and garlic with masher or electric mixer, adding milk and margarine. Season to taste with salt and pepper.

3. Spoon potatoes onto plates; spoon vegetables over potatoes.

Nutritional Data

PER SERVING		EXCHANGES	
Calories:	451	Milk:	0.0
% Calories from fat:	13	Vegetable:	5.0
Fat (gm):	6.9	Fruit:	0.0
Sat. fat (gm):	1.3	Bread:	4.0
Cholesterol (mg):	0.3	Meat:	0.0
Sodium (mg):	227	Fat:	1.0
Protein (gm):	13.1		
Carbohydrate (gm):	90.8		

ROASTED SQUASH, MOROCCAN STYLE

Roasted vegetables and pineapple, combined with couscous, create a perfect filling for oven-roasted acorn squash.

Serves 4 (about 2 cups each)

Olive oil cooking spray

2 medium acorn squash, cut in halves, seeded

1 medium pineapple, peeled, cored, cut in 1-inch chunks

2 medium onions, sliced

2 cups quartered Brussels sprouts

1/4 cup (packed) light brown sugar

Pinch dried cinnamon

Pinch ground nutmeg

1/2 cup frozen whole-kernel corn, cooked, drained

1/4 cup dark raisins

1/4 cup finely chopped cilantro leaves

2/3 cup couscous, cooked

Salt, to taste

Pepper, to taste

1. Spray aluminum-foil-lined jellyroll pan with cooking spray. Place squash halves, pineapple, onions, and Brussels sprouts on pan in single layer; spray generously with cooking spray. Sprinkle squash with brown sugar, cinnamon, and nutmeg. Bake at 400 degrees until vegetables are tender, about 40 minutes. Reserve squash halves.

2. Stir roasted vegetables, corn, raisins, and cilantro into couscous; season to taste with salt and pepper. Spoon couscous mixture into squash halves and serve.

Nutritional Data

PER SERVING		EXCHANGES	
Calories:	450	Milk:	0.0
% Calories from fat:	3	Vegetable:	2.5
Fat (gm):	1.5	Fruit:	1.5
Sat. fat (gm):	0.2	Bread:	4.0
Cholesterol (mg):	0	Meat:	0.0
Sodium (mg):	49	Fat:	0.0
Protein (gm):	11.8		
Carbohydrate (gm):	107		

GRILL-ROASTED VEGETABLES WITH POLENTA

◆

The vegetables can also be oven-roasted at 400 degrees for 30–40 minutes. For convenience, the polenta can be made 2–3 days in advance.

Serves 4 (about 1½ cups each)

2 medium eggplants, unpeeled, cut in ½-inch rounds
4 medium tomatoes, cut in wedges
4 medium red onions, cut in wedges
2 medium red bell peppers, cut in 1-inch slices
2 medium yellow summer squash, cut in 1-inch pieces
2 large bulbs garlic, tops trimmed
   Vegetable cooking spray
2 tablespoons balsamic, *or* red wine, vinegar
1 tablespoon olive oil, *or* vegetable oil
1 teaspoon lemon juice

    1/2 teaspoon dried rosemary
    1/2 teaspoon dried sage
    1/2 teaspoon dried thyme
        Polenta (recipe follows)
    4 slices Italian bread, toasted

1. Spray vegetables, including garlic, with cooking spray; place on grill over medium-hot coals. Grill, turning occasionally, until vegetables are browned and tender, about 30 minutes. Combine vegetables, except garlic, in bowl. Mix vinegar, oil, lemon juice, and herbs; drizzle over vegetables and toss.

2. Spray large skillet with cooking spray; heat on grill or range until hot. Cut Polenta into 8 wedges; cook in skillet until browned on both sides. Overlap 2 polenta wedges on each serving plate; spoon dressed vegetables over.

3. Separate each garlic bulb into 2 pieces. Squeeze garlic from cloves to spread on bread.

Polenta

        Vegetable cooking spray
    2 green onions, green and white parts, sliced
    1 clove garlic, minced
    1 teaspoon dried basil
    1 can (14 1/2 ounces) vegetable broth
    1/2 cup water
    3/4 cup yellow cornmeal
    1/2 teaspoon salt

1. Spray large saucepan with cooking spray; heat over medium heat until hot. Saute onions, garlic, and basil until tender, about 5 minutes. Add broth and water and heat to boiling; gradually stir in cornmeal and salt. Cook over low heat, stirring constantly, until thickened, about 10 minutes.

2. Pour into lightly greased 8-inch cake pan; cool to room temperature. Refrigerate, lightly covered, until polenta is firm, 3–4 hours.

Nutritional Data

PER SERVING		EXCHANGES	
Calories:	374	Milk:	0.0
% Calories from fat:	15	Vegetable:	6.0
Fat (gm):	6.6	Fruit:	0.0
Sat. fat (gm):	1	Bread:	2.5
Cholesterol (mg):	0	Meat:	0.0
Sodium (mg):	512	Fat:	1.0
Protein (gm):	10		
Carbohydrate (gm):	74.3		

VEGGIE POCKET SANDWICHES

Delicious as a sandwich with sourdough or multigrain bread also!

Serves 4

Vegetable cooking spray
1 medium eggplant, unpeeled, cut in 1-inch cubes
1 large sweet potato, unpeeled, cut in ½-inch slices
1 medium green bell pepper, cut in ¾-inch slices
1 large onion, sliced
1 large tomato, cut in 8 wedges
2 tablespoons balsamic, *or* red wine, vinegar
1 tablespoon olive oil, *or* vegetable oil
1 teaspoon lemon juice
2 cloves garlic, minced
1 teaspoon dried oregano
1 teaspoon dried basil
Salt, to taste
Pepper, to taste
4 pita pockets, cut in halves

1. Spray aluminum-foil-lined jellyroll pan with cooking spray. Arrange vegetables on pan in single layer and spray generously with cooking spray. Bake at 400 degrees until vegetables are browned and tender, about 30 minutes. Combine vegetables in bowl.

2. Combine vinegar, oil, lemon juice, garlic, oregano, and basil; drizzle over vegetables and toss. Season to taste with salt and pepper. Spoon dressed vegetables into pita pockets.

Nutritional Data

PER SERVING		EXCHANGES	
Calories:	292	Milk:	0.0
% Calories from fat:	14	Vegetable:	3.0
Fat (gm):	4.6	Fruit:	0.0
Sat. fat (gm):	0.6	Bread:	2.5
Cholesterol (mg):	0	Meat:	0.0
Sodium (mg):	334	Fat:	1.0
Protein (gm):	7.9		
Carbohydrate (gm):	56.3		

7
CASSEROLES AND LOAVES

Broccoli, Spinach, and Noodle Casserole

Sweet-and-Sour Cabbage Casserole with Barley

Roasted Eggplant and Cream Cheese Casserole

Spinach-Noodle Casserole

Tian

Cabbage Custard with Basil-Tomato Sauce

Eggplant Parmesan

Old Fashioned Garden Vegetable Pudding

Old Fashioned Corn, Tomato, and Cheese Pudding

Baked Vegetable Loaf

Succotash Loaf

Broccoli, Cauliflower, and Cheese Loaf

Hearty Bulgur Loaf

BROCCOLI, SPINACH, AND NOODLE CASSEROLE

This casserole uses what looks like a lot of reduced-calorie margarine, but when examined in context, the rest of the ingredients contain so little fat that the recipe comes in well within the guidelines for daily fat consumption.

Serves 8

  3 packages (10 ounces each) frozen chopped spinach, thawed

  2 packages (10 ounces each) frozen chopped broccoli, thawed

 13 tablespoons reduced-calorie margarine (divided)

  2 cups finely minced red onions

$3/4$ cup plus 2 tablespoons evaporated skim milk

  1 cup egg substitute

  4 egg whites

$1/4$ cup flour

  1 teaspoon salt (optional) (divided)

  1 teaspoon ground nutmeg

$3/4$ teaspoon white pepper

  6 cups cooked medium-size noodles, drained (divided)

$1 1/3$ cups breadcrumbs, made from reduced-calorie white bread.

1. Preheat oven to 350 degrees. Place spinach in colander and press to extract liquid until spinach is very dry. Place broccoli in colander and press to extract liquid until very dry.

2. Melt 2 tablespoons margarine in nonstick skillet over medium heat; saute onions 5 minutes. Use spatula to scrape onions and all remaining fat into bowl of electric mixer.

3. Melt 7 tablespoons margarine and spoon into bowl with onions. Add milk, egg substitute, egg whites, flour, (optional) $3/4$ teaspoon salt, nutmeg, and pepper. Beat until combined. Add spinach and beat again. Add broccoli and beat again.

4. If desired, sprinkle ¼ teaspoon salt into noodles and toss to combine. Spoon 2 cups noodles into 9 x 13-inch glass casserole. Spoon half the broccoli-spinach mixture (3 cups) over noodles.

5. Continue layering, using 2 cups noodles and remaining broccoli-spinach mixture next, and spooning remaining 2 cups noodles on top of casserole.

6. Melt remaining ¼ cup margarine. Combine with breadcrumbs and sprinkle over top of casserole.

7. Bake 35 minutes or until crumbs are lightly browned. Remove from oven and let rest 15 minutes. Cut in half lengthwise, then cut each half into 4 pieces.

Nutritional Data

PER SERVING		EXCHANGES	
Calories:	376	Milk:	0.0
% Calories from fat:	28	Vegetable:	2.0
Fat (gm):	11.8	Fruit:	0.0
Sat. fat (gm):	2.2	Bread:	2.5
Cholesterol (mg):	40.6	Meat:	1.0
Sodium (mg):	706	Fat:	2.0
Protein (gm):	18.1		
Carbohydrate (gm):	51.6		

SWEET-AND-SOUR CABBAGE CASSEROLE WITH BARLEY

Serves 6

1 can (1 pound) peeled tomatoes, coarsely chopped, with liquid
1 small onion, quartered
6 tablespoons lemon juice
1/4 cup sugar
1/4 teaspoon salt
1 bay leaf, halved
1/8 teaspoon ground cloves
1 1/4 cups water
1 cabbage (3 pounds), cut in 1/2-inch slices
1/2 cup raisins
6 tablespoons gingersnap crumbs (made in food processor or blender)
4 1/2 cups cooked barley, hot

1. Preheat oven to 300 degrees. Place tomatoes and liquid in medium saucepan. Add onion, lemon juice, sugar, salt, bay leaf, cloves, and water. Heat to boiling and remove from heat.

2. Place half the sliced cabbage in ovenproof casserole with cover. Pour half the sauce over cabbage. Arrange remaining cabbage over sauce and spoon remaining sauce over cabbage. Add cover or top with foil. Bake 1 hour.

3. Open casserole, sprinkle raisins and crumbs into liquid, and press and swirl to combine. Cover as before and bake 1 more hour.

4. Bring casserole to table. Spoon 3/4 cup barley onto each of 6 dinner plates. Spoon cabbage and sauce over barley, dividing it evenly. Serve immediately.

Nutritional Data

PER SERVING		EXCHANGES	
Calories:	310	Milk:	0.0
% Calories from fat:	5	Vegetable:	3.0
Fat (gm):	2	Fruit:	0.5
Sat. fat (gm):	0.3	Bread:	3.0
Cholesterol (mg):	0	Meat:	0.0
Sodium (mg):	300	Fat:	0.0
Protein (gm):	6.4		
Carbohydrate (gm):	72.2		

ROASTED EGGPLANT AND CREAM CHEESE CASSEROLE

Serves 4

2 pounds baby eggplants, cut in 1/2-inch slices
  Olive oil cooking spray
1/4 teaspoon salt (optional)
1 teaspoon dried thyme (divided)
1 teaspoon canola oil
1/2 teaspoon minced garlic
1/2 cup chopped red onion
2/3 cup chopped red bell pepper
6 tablespoons pitted, coarsely chopped kalamata olives*
1 can (16 ounces) low-sodium peeled tomatoes with liquid, coarsely chopped
1/4 cup water
2 tablespoons sodium-free tomato paste
1/2 teaspoon dried oregano
1/8 teaspoon pepper
1 cup fat-free cream cheese (not tub type)
1/4 cup evaporated skim milk

1. Preheat broiler. Place oven rack near broiler. Line cookie sheet with baking parchment and lay eggplant slices on parchment; spray lightly with olive-oil-flavored cooking spray. Mix (optional) salt and 1/2 teaspoon thyme, and sprinkle half this mixture onto eggplant.

2. Broil eggplant 5 minutes on one side. Turn with spatula, spray again, and sprinkle with remaining (optional) salt and thyme mixture. Broil 4–5 minutes more (watch carefully) or until lightly browned and fork-tender.

3. Preheat oven to 350 degrees. Heat canola oil in nonstick skillet over medium heat and saute garlic 1 minute. Add onion and bell pepper and saute 4 minutes more. Add olives and saute 1 minute more.

4. Arrange layer of eggplant, using half the slices, on bottom of a 7 1/2 x 11-inch glass casserole (or any equivalent baking dish). Overlap or cut eggplant slices if necessary to cover bottom completely.

5. Spoon olive mixture over eggplant. Top with remaining eggplant slices, cutting some to fit empty spaces as before.

6. Empty chopped tomatoes with liquid into saucepan. Add ¼ cup water, tomato paste, oregano, pepper, and remaining ½ teaspoon thyme. Heat to boil and pour over casserole.

7. Bake 20 minutes. Mix cream cheese and skim milk. Use spatula to spread cream cheese over top of casserole, working from edges inward. Return to oven for 10 minutes more.

*Note: If necessary, substitute another type of Middle Eastern or Mediterranean brined olive; do not substitute regular black or green olives.

Nutritional Data

PER SERVING		EXCHANGES	
Calories:	225	Milk:	0.0
% Calories from fat:	25	Vegetable:	6.0
Fat (gm):	6.6	Fruit:	0.0
Sat. fat (gm):	0.8	Bread:	0.0
Cholesterol (mg):	10.5	Meat:	0.5
Sodium (mg):	803	Fat:	1.0
Protein (gm):	13.5		
Carbohydrate (gm):	30.1		

SPINACH-NOODLE CASSEROLE

Serves 4

4 packages (10 ounces each) frozen chopped spinach, thawed

12 sun-dried tomatoes

¼ cup reduced-calorie margarine (divided)

1¼ cups minced onions

½ teaspoon white pepper

1 teaspoon salt (divided) (optional)

½ cup egg substitute

3 cups cooked spinach noodles, drained

1 cup breadcrumbs, blender-made from reduced-calorie white bread

¼ cup (1 ounce) minced reduced-calorie Colby cheese, *or* Monterey Jack *or* Swiss

1. Preheat oven to 350 degrees. Place spinach in colander and press hard until all liquid is extracted and spinach is dry.

2. Place tomatoes in saucepan with water to cover; heat to boiling. Remove from heat, and let steep until softened, about 15 minutes. Chop tomatoes and reserve.

3. Melt 2 tablespoons margarine in large nonstick skillet. Add onions and chopped tomatoes and saute 5 minutes. Add pepper and (optional) 1/2 teaspoon salt.

4. Transfer onion-tomato mixture to bowl, using scraper to get all pan margarine into bowl. Add spinach and mix very well. Stir in egg substitute.

5. In separate bowl, combine noodles and remaining (optional) 1/2 teaspoon salt. Melt 1 tablespoon margarine and add to noodles, tossing well.

6. Spoon 1 cup noodles onto bottom of 11 x 7 1/2-inch glass baking dish or 2-quart casserole. Spoon half of spinach mixture over noodles.

7. Repeat layers, using another cup of noodles and remaining spinach mixture. Top casserole with remaining 1 cup noodles.

8. Combine crumbs with cheese. Cut in remaining 1 tablespoon margarine to make streusel. Sprinkle over top layer of noodles. Bake 30 minutes. Cut into quarters to serve.

Nutritional Data

PER SERVING		EXCHANGES	
Calories:	405	Milk:	0.0
% Calories from fat:	20	Vegetable:	2.0
Fat (gm):	9.8	Fruit:	0.0
Sat. fat (gm):	2.3	Bread:	3.5
Cholesterol (mg):	44.1	Meat:	1.0
Sodium (mg):	458	Fat:	1.0
Protein (gm):	20.1		
Carbohydrate (gm):	65.3		

TIAN

This lovely casserole can be served hot. But it's so good cold that we can recommend it for an August day.

Serves 6 (about 1½ cups each)

2 cups boiling water
8 ounces dried small white beans (navy or Great Northern)
1 vegetable bouillon cube
5 yellow summer squash, cut into ⅓-inch slices
5 small zucchini, cut into ⅓-inch slices
2 tablespoons canola oil
2 large tomatoes, peeled, seeded, chopped
1 package (10 ounces) frozen (thawed) chopped spinach, drained
3–4 cloves garlic, minced
¼ teaspoon dried rosemary leaves
¼ teaspoon ground nutmeg
1 teaspoon salt
½ teaspoon pepper
¾ cup grated Parmesan cheese
¾ cup fresh white breadcrumbs
½ cup finely chopped parsley leaves
¼ teaspoon paprika

1. Pour boiling water over beans in large saucepan; add bouillon cube, stirring to dissolve. Let stand 8 hours or until water is absorbed. Add enough water to just cover beans and heat to boiling; reduce heat and simmer, covered, until beans are tender, 40–60 minutes, adding more water if necessary. Drain beans and transfer to 2 1/2-quart casserole.

2. Arrange squash and zucchini in greased foil-lined roasting pan; brush with oil. Bake at 350 degrees until tender, about 30 minutes; add to beans with tomatoes, spinach, garlic, rosemary, nutmeg, salt, and pepper, mixing well.

3. Sprinkle top of casserole with combined Parmesan cheese, breadcrumbs, parsley, and paprika. Bake at 350 degrees until topping is browned, about 20 minutes.

Nutritional Data

PER SERVING		EXCHANGES	
Calories:	322	Milk:	0.0
% Calories from fat:	26	Vegetable:	3.0
Fat (gm):	10	Fruit:	0.0
Sat. fat (gm):	3	Bread:	2.0
Cholesterol (mg):	9.9	Meat:	0.5
Sodium (mg):	817	Fat:	1.5
Protein (gm):	17.9		
Carbohydrate (gm):	44.8		

CABBAGE CUSTARD WITH BASIL-TOMATO SAUCE

Serves 6

Basil-Tomato Sauce

1 vegetable bouillon cube
1 cup boiling water
1 tablespoon canola oil
1 clove garlic, minced
1 cup minced red bell pepper
1/4 cup minced red onion
2 large tomatoes, peeled, seeded, chopped
1 teaspoon dried basil
1 teaspoon dried oregano (optional)

Custard

2 tablespoons reduced-calorie margarine
6 cups coarsely chopped cabbage
1 cup dry white wine
1 1/4 cups egg substitute, *or* 5 eggs
2 cups evaporated skim milk
1 teaspoon ground nutmeg
1/3 teaspoon salt
1/4 teaspoon white pepper

1. Make basil-tomato sauce: Combine bouillon cube and boiling water to make broth.

2. Heat oil in medium nonstick skillet over medium heat. Saute garlic 1 minute. Add bell pepper and onion and saute 5 minutes more or until vegetables are tender. Add tomatoes, basil, and (optional) oregano and saute 3 minutes more.

3. Measure out 3/4 cup vegetable broth and add to skillet. Heat to boiling, then reduce heat to simmer. Cook, uncovered, until sauce thickens, about 10 minutes. Sauce should measure about 2 2/3 cups.

4. Make custard: Preheat oven to 350 degrees. Melt margarine in large skillet over medium heat. Add cabbage and cook, stirring often, about 5 minutes. Add wine and simmer, uncovered, until cabbage is tender and all liquid has evaporated completely, about 20 minutes.

5. Beat egg substitute with milk. Stir in nutmeg, salt, and pepper. Add to cabbage and stir to combine. Spoon into 10 x 8-inch casserole. Bake 20–25 minutes or until just barely firm in center.

6. Bring cabbage custard to table cut in wedges. Spoon a scant 1/2 cup heated sauce over each custard wedge.

Nutritional Data

PER SERVING		EXCHANGES	
Calories:	220	Milk:	1.0
% Calories from fat:	27	Vegetable:	2.0
Fat (gm):	6.7	Fruit:	0.0
Sat. fat (gm):	1.1	Bread:	0.0
Cholesterol (mg):	3.2	Meat:	1.0
Sodium (mg):	542	Fat:	0.5
Protein (gm):	14.8		
Carbohydrate (gm):	20.2		

EGGPLANT PARMESAN

Serves 4

2 pounds baby eggplant, cut in ½-inch slices (divided)
¼ teaspoon salt
1 teaspoon dried oregano (divided)
1 teaspoon reduced-calorie margarine
1½ teaspoons minced garlic
⅔ cup minced red onion
2¼ pounds canned peeled Italian plum tomatoes with liquid, chopped
1½ teaspoons sugar
1 teaspoon dried basil
⅛ teaspoon pepper
1 bay leaf
14 tablespoons grated reduced-fat mozzarella cheese (divided)
2 tablespoons grated Parmesan, *or* Romano, cheese (divided) (do not use pre-grated)

1. Preheat oven to 350 degrees. Line large cookie sheet with baking parchment. Arrange eggplant slices on parchment and brush with water. Sprinkle salt and ½ teaspoon oregano over eggplant. Bake 15 minutes. Turn with spatula and bake another 15 minutes.

2. Heat margarine in nonstick skillet over medium heat. Saute garlic 1 minute. Add onion and saute 3–4 minutes more. Spoon skillet contents into large saucepan.

3. Add chopped tomatoes and liquid, sugar, basil, pepper, bay leaf, and remaining ½ teaspoon oregano to saucepan. Simmer over medium heat 20 minutes or until mixture measures about 2⅔ cups.

4. Arrange half of eggplant on bottom of 8 x 10-inch casserole. Quarter slices to fill empty spaces. Spoon half the tomato sauce (1⅓ cups) over eggplant. Sprinkle 6 tablespoons mozzarella over sauce. Sprinkle 1 tablespoon Parmesan over mozzarella. Arrange a second layer of eggplant slices over cheeses and top with remaining tomato sauce, 8 tablespoons mozzarella, and 1 tablespoon Parmesan.

5. Bake, uncovered, 25–30 minutes or until cheeses are melted and sauce bubbles. Remove bay leaf. Let rest in casserole 10 minutes before serving.

Optional: If desired, pass Parmesan wedge and grater on serving plate so guests can grate additional cheese onto their servings.

Nutritional Data

PER SERVING		EXCHANGES	
Calories:	220	Milk:	0.0
% Calories from fat:	24	Vegetable:	6.0
Fat (gm):	6.2	Fruit:	0.0
Sat. fat (gm):	3.6	Bread:	0.0
Cholesterol (mg):	16.9	Meat:	1.0
Sodium (mg):	787	Fat:	0.5
Protein (gm):	12.9		
Carbohydrate (gm):	31.0		

OLD FASHIONED GARDEN VEGETABLE PUDDING

Although egg whites are folded into this mild, comforting dish, it's not a soufflé. It's baked in a hot water bath in the oven and will not fall when brought to the table.

Serves 4

⅔ cup (packed) coarsely chopped frozen cauliflower florets, thawed

⅔ cup (packed) coarsely chopped frozen broccoli, thawed

⅔ cup frozen peas

⅔ cup peeled, quartered baby carrots

⅔ cup frozen corn

2 tablespoons reduced-calorie margarine

½ cup minced red onion

2 tablespoons flour

1 cup evaporated skim milk

½ teaspoon salt

¼ teaspoon ground nutmeg plus 1 large pinch

¼ teaspoon white pepper

1 cup egg substitute

5 large egg whites (about ⅔ cup)

1 teaspoon cream of tartar

2 teaspoons sugar

1. Preheat oven to 350 degrees. Place large roasting pan in oven. Add boiling water to depth of about 1 inch.

2. In 2 inches simmering water, heat cauliflower, broccoli, peas, and carrots until tender, about 5 minutes. Add corn, turn off heat, and let rest 2 minutes.

3. Drain vegetables in colander under cold running tap water to stop cooking. Place vegetables in bowl.

4. Melt 2 tablespoons margarine over medium heat in large saucepan. Add onion and saute 3–4 minutes. Add flour and cook, stirring constantly with wire whisk, about 30 seconds or until combined. Add milk slowly, stirring constantly with whisk. Add salt, nutmeg, and pepper and simmer until thick, 2–3 minutes. Allow sauce to cool.

5. Stir egg substitute into milk mixture. Then add vegetables and toss to combine.

6. Beat egg whites until they hold soft peaks. Add cream of tartar and beat until they hold stiff peaks. With beaters running, add sugar and beat until very stiff but not dry. Fold egg whites into vegetables.

7. Spoon pudding into large ovenproof glass baking dish with lots of surface area. (Do not use soufflé dish.) Place in oven in hot water bath. Bake 40–45 minutes or until lightly browned on top. Serve immediately from casserole.

Nutritional Data

PER SERVING		EXCHANGES	
Calories:	215	Milk:	0.5
% Calories from fat:	14	Vegetable:	1.0
Fat (gm):	3.3	Fruit:	0.0
Sat. fat (gm):	0.7	Bread:	1.0
Cholesterol (mg):	2	Meat:	1.5
Sodium (mg):	598	Fat:	0.0
Protein (gm):	18.2		
Carbohydrate (gm):	29		

Old Fashioned Corn, Tomato, and Cheese Pudding

Serves 4

1 cup egg substitute, *or* 4 eggs
2 cups evaporated skim milk
2 tablespoons reduced-calorie margarine, melted
¼ cup flour
¼ teaspoon salt
½ teaspoon sugar
⅛ teaspoon white pepper
½ cup skinned, seeded, chopped tomato, pressed in colander to extract liquid
1 cup frozen corn, thawed
½ cup (2 ounces) grated reduced-calorie Colby cheese
1 tablespoon minced red onion

1. Heat oven to 325 degrees. Place large pan with raised sides in oven. Add boiling water to a depth of about 1 inch.

2. In medium bowl, beat egg substitute with milk and margarine. Beat in flour, salt, sugar, and pepper. Add tomato, corn, cheese, and onion to egg mixture.

3. Spoon into a shallow 6-cup casserole, about 8 x 11 inches. Place casserole in pan containing water. Bake 50 minutes or until top is firm.

Nutritional Data

PER SERVING		EXCHANGES	
Calories:	262	Milk:	1.0
% Calories from fat:	20	Vegetable:	0.5
Fat (gm):	5.8	Fruit:	0.0
Sat. fat (gm):	2.2	Bread:	1.0
Cholesterol (mg):	14.1	Meat:	2.0
Sodium (mg):	545	Fat:	0.0
Protein (gm):	21.7		
Carbohydrate (gm):	32		

BAKED VEGETABLE LOAF

The scallion-cilantro topping is an important flavor element in this pretty loaf, which can be eaten hot or cold.

Serves 4

- 2 teaspoons reduced-calorie margarine
- 1/3 cup chopped red onion
- 1 1/4 pounds yellow squash, peeled, cut in chunks
- 1 cup egg substitute (divided) *or* 4 eggs
- 2/3 cup evaporated skim milk (divided)
- 4 teaspoons flour (divided)
- 3/4 teaspoon salt (divided)
- 1/4 teaspoon white pepper (divided)
- 1/2 cup frozen corn, thawed
- 1 package (10 ounces) frozen chopped broccoli, thawed (divided)
- 1/8 teaspoon dried thyme
- 1/8 teaspoon dried sage
- 1/8 teaspoon ground nutmeg
- 1 tablespoon minced green onion, green part only
- 1 tablespoon minced cilantro leaves

1. Preheat oven to 350 degrees. Line bottom of 8 1/2 x 4 1/2-inch bread pan with cooking parchment.

2. Melt margarine in nonstick skillet over medium heat and saute onion 3–4 minutes. Reserve.

3. Place squash in saucepan and cover with water. Boil 5–6 minutes or until fork tender. Drain in colander. Press to extract liquid.

4. Place squash, 1/2 cup egg substitute, 1/3 cup milk, 2 teaspoons flour, 1/2 teaspoon salt, and 1/8 teaspoon white pepper in food processor or blender container. Puree until smooth. Mix with corn kernels.

5. Place 1 cup broccoli, remaining 1/2 cup egg substitute, 1/3 cup milk, 2 teaspoons flour, 1/4 teaspoon salt, 1/8 teaspoon white pepper, thyme, sage, and nutmeg in food processor or blender container. Puree until smooth. Transfer to bowl. Stir in reserved sauteed onion and remaining chopped broccoli.

6. Spoon half the squash mixture into prepared pan. Carefully spoon broccoli mixture over squash. Top with remaining squash mixture. Bake 90 minutes.

7. Run a knife blade thoroughly between loaf and pan on all sides. Invert on serving plate to remove.

8. Combine green onions and cilantro. Spoon mixture on top of loaf, down the center, at serving time.

Nutritional Data

PER SERVING		EXCHANGES	
Calories:	161	Milk:	0.5
% Calories from fat:	18	Vegetable:	2.0
Fat (gm):	3.5	Fruit:	0.0
Sat. fat (gm):	0.7	Bread:	0.5
Cholesterol (mg):	1.3	Meat:	0.5
Sodium (mg):	617	Fat:	0.5
Protein (gm):	12.8		
Carbohydrate (gm):	22.4		

SUCCOTASH LOAF

◆

Serves 4

Lima Layer

Vegetable cooking spray
2 tablespoons reduced-calorie margarine
1/4 cup minced onion
1 1/2 cups frozen baby lima beans, thawed, drained (divided)
1/2 cup plus 2 tablespoons egg substitute
1/4 cup evaporated skim milk
1/4 teaspoon salt
1/8 teaspoon white pepper
1/2 cup reduced-calorie breadcrumbs
2 tablespoons minced parsley leaves

Corn Layer

5 sun-dried tomatoes
1 1/2 cups frozen corn kernels, thawed, drained (divided)
1/2 cup reduced-calorie breadcrumbs
1/2 cup plus 2 tablespoons egg substitute
1/4 cup evaporated skim milk
2 tablespoons reduced-calorie margarine, melted

　　1 tablespoon flour
　　½ teaspoon sugar
　　¼ teaspoon salt
　　⅛ teaspoon white pepper
　　　 Parsley sprigs (optional)

1. Preheat oven to 350 degrees. Spray bottom and sides of metal, 8½ x 4½-inch bread pan with vegetable cooking spray, and line bottom with parchment. Place large pan with raised sides in oven, adding boiling water to depth of 1 inch.

2. Make lima layer: Melt margarine over medium heat in nonstick skillet. Add onion and saute 3 minutes.

3. Place ½ cup lima beans in food processor with egg substitute, milk, salt, and white pepper. Process until coarsely pureed.

4. Spoon puree into bowl. Stir in breadcrumbs, parsley, and remaining 1 cup limas. Add onions and margarine to bowl, mixing well. Spoon into prepared bread pan. Place pan in water-filled larger pan in oven. Bake 30 minutes.

5. Make corn layer: Cover tomatoes with boiling water and let stand 5 minutes. Drain and chop tomatoes, and place in bowl with 1 cup corn and breadcrumbs.

6. Place remaining ½ cup corn in food processor container with egg substitute, milk, margarine, flour, sugar, salt, and pepper. Process until coarsely pureed. Add to corn and tomatoes and mix well.

7. Carefully spoon corn mixture over baked lima layer in pan. Return to oven and bake another 45 minutes or until top is firm.

8. Carefully run a knife blade along inside of pan to loosen loaf. Invert onto a serving plate. Garnish with parsley. Serve immediately.

Nutritional Data

PER SERVING		EXCHANGES	
Calories:	320	Milk:	0.5
% Calories from fat:	17	Vegetable:	0.0
Fat (gm):	6.6	Fruit:	0.0
Sat. fat (gm):	1.2	Bread:	3.0
Cholesterol (mg):	1	Meat:	1.0
Sodium (mg):	640	Fat:	0.5
Protein (gm):	18.6		
Carbohydrate (gm):	51.1		

BROCCOLI, CAULIFLOWER, AND CHEESE LOAF

Serves 4

6 sun-dried tomatoes (divided)
2 tablespoons reduced-calorie margarine
1 cup minced red onion
1¼ cups egg substitute (divided)
¼ cup evaporated skim milk (divided)
¾ teaspoon salt (divided)
¼ teaspoon white pepper (divided)
4 large pinches ground nutmeg (divided)
2 cups cooked chopped broccoli, fresh *or* frozen, drained
2 cups cooked chopped cauliflower, fresh *or* frozen, drained
1 cup crumbs from reduced-calorie bread (divided)
¼ cup grated reduced-calorie Colby cheese
2 tablespoons chopped parsley leaves
2 tablespoons grated reduced-calorie Colby cheese

1. Preheat oven to 325 degrees. Line a 9 x 5-inch bread pan on bottom with cooking parchment. Place dried tomatoes in bowl and cover with boiling water. Let rest 10 minutes.

2. Heat margarine over medium heat in nonstick skillet. Add onion and saute 5 minutes, stirring often with wooden spoon.

3. Place ½ cup plus 2 tablespoons egg substitute into each of 2 bowls. Add 2 tablespoons milk, ⅜ teaspoon salt, ⅛ teaspoon pepper, and 2 pinches nutmeg to each bowl. Mix each well.

4. Drain and mince tomatoes and spoon half into each bowl. Spoon half of onions into each bowl. Mix well.

5. Press broccoli in colander to extract excess liquid and add to first bowl. Press cauliflower in colander to extract excess liquid and add to second bowl. Stir ½ cup breadcrumbs and ¼ cup cheese into each bowl.

6. Spoon cauliflower mixture into prepared pan. Spoon broccoli mixture over cauliflower. Bake 70–80 minutes or until top is lightly browned and firm. Run a knife blade around inside of pan to loosen loaf.

7. Invert pan carefully onto serving plate and slowly lift pan. Combine parsley and grated cheese and sprinkle over top of loaf.

Nutritional Data

PER SERVING		EXCHANGES	
Calories:	250	Milk:	0.0
% Calories from fat:	23	Vegetable:	4.0
Fat (gm):	6.9	Fruit:	0.0
Sat. fat (gm):	2.6	Bread:	0.5
Cholesterol (mg):	13.2	Meat:	2.0
Sodium (mg):	771	Fat:	0.0
Protein (gm):	19.6		
Carbohydrate (gm):	31.4		

HEARTY BULGUR LOAF

An interesting combination of bulgur and grits, the loaf mixture can also be formed into patties, coated with unseasoned bread-crumbs, and sauteed in a lightly greased skillet. Herb-Tomato Sauce (see Index) is also delicious served with the loaf or patties.

Serves 6

¹/₃ cup bulgur
¹/₂ cup cold water
 1 cup cooked grits
 2 cups unseasoned breadcrumbs
 1 medium onion, finely chopped
 1 cup frozen thawed, whole-kernel corn
 2 medium carrots, finely chopped
 1 medium green bell pepper, finely chopped
 1 can (8 ounces) reduced-sodium tomato sauce
 2 eggs, beaten
 1 teaspoon dried cumin
¹/₂ teaspoon dried marjoram
¹/₂ teaspoon salt
¹/₄ teaspoon pepper
 2 cups Cucumber Yogurt (see pg. 48)

1. Heat bulgur and water to boiling in small saucepan; remove from heat and let stand until tender, about 15 minutes. Drain bulgur and mix, in large bowl, with remaining ingredients, except Cucumber Yogurt. Pack mixture into lightly greased 8¹/₂ x 4¹/₂ x 2¹/₂-inch loaf pan.

2. Bake at 350 degrees until browned on top, about 45 minutes. Loosen edges of loaf with pancake turner; invert onto serving plate. Slice and serve with Cucumber Yogurt.

Nutritional Data

PER SERVING		EXCHANGES	
Calories:	305	Milk:	0.0
% Calories from fat:	12	Vegetable:	2.0
Fat (gm):	4.1	Fruit:	0.0
Sat. fat (gm):	1.1	Bread:	3.0
Cholesterol (mg):	71.9	Meat:	0.0
Sodium (mg):	572	Fat:	1.0
Protein (gm):	13.3		
Carbohydrate (gm):	54.8		

8
EGG AND DAIRY DISHES

Black Bean Cheesecake with Salsa

Sweet Potato Pone

Mushroom Custard in Acorn Squash

Eggs Rancheros with Black Beans and 2 Salsas

Breakfast Burritos

Vegetable Frittata with Parmesan Toast

Omelet Puff with Vegetable Mélange

Onion Quiche

Spinach, Onion, and Cheese Quiche

Egg and Cheese Casserole

BLACK BEAN CHEESECAKE WITH SALSA

This unusual entree can also be served in smaller pieces as an appetizer or first course. It can also be served at room temperature, rather than heating as the recipe directs. Make it a day in advance, as overnight chilling is essential.

Serves 8

  4 flour tortillas
  3 packages (8 ounces each) fat-free cream
     cheese (not tub type), room temperature
1½ cups cholesterol-free egg substitute, *or* 6 eggs
  1 can (15 ounces) black beans, rinsed, drained
  ½ jalapeño pepper, finely chopped
  2 tablespoons finely chopped onion
  2 cloves garlic, minced
  2 teaspoons Worcestershire sauce
  2 teaspoons dried cumin
  ½ teaspoon dried oregano
  ½ teaspoon chili powder
  ½ teaspoon salt (optional)
  ½ teaspoon cayenne
     Vegetable cooking spray
     Fresh Tomato Salsa (see pg. 108), salt withheld

1. Lightly grease 9-inch springform pan and line with overlapping tortillas.

2. Beat cream cheese in large bowl until fluffy; beat in egg substitute. Mix in remaining ingredients, except cooking spray and Salsa. Bake at 300 degrees until center is set and sharp knife inserted halfway between center and edge of cheesecake comes out almost clean, 1¾–2 hours. Cool to room temperature on wire rack. Refrigerate overnight.

3. Spray large skillet with cooking spray; heat over medium heat until hot. Cook wedges of cheesecake over medium-low heat until browned on both sides. Serve with Tomato Salsa.

Nutritional Data

PER SERVING		EXCHANGES	
Calories:	205	Milk:	0.5
% Calories from fat:	7	Vegetable:	0.5
Fat (gm):	1.5	Fruit:	0.0
Sat. fat (gm):	0.2	Bread:	1.5
Cholesterol (mg):	15	Meat:	1.0
Sodium (mg):	756	Fat:	0.0
Protein (gm):	22.3		
Carbohydrate (gm):	25.8		

SWEET POTATO PONE

More of a country-style pudding than a soufflé, this comfort food will become a favorite. Drizzle with warm maple syrup, if you like, and serve with a favorite vegetable and salad of crisp greens.

Serves 2

     1 small onion, finely chopped
     1 tablespoon margarine
     3 tablespoons flour
     1 cup skim milk
    ½ cup cholesterol-free egg substitute, *or* 2 eggs
     1 large sweet potato (about 8 ounces), unpeeled,
        cut into 1-inch cubes, cooked
     2 tablespoons (packed) light brown sugar
    ¼ teaspoon dried cinnamon
    ⅛ teaspoon ground nutmeg
    ⅛ teaspoon ground cloves
    ¼ teaspoon salt
    2–3 dashes white pepper
     4 egg whites, beaten to stiff peaks

1. Saute onion in margarine in saucepan until tender, 3–5 minutes. Stir in flour; cook 2–3 minutes. Stir in milk; heat to boil, stirring constantly, until thickened.

2. Beat egg substitute in small bowl until thick and lemon colored, 2–3 minutes. Slowly beat about half the milk mixture into egg; then stir egg mixture into milk mixture in saucepan. Cook over low heat, stirring constantly, 1–2 minutes. Remove from heat.

3. Coarsely mash sweet potato with fork. Mix sweet potato, brown sugar, spices, salt, and pepper into milk mixture. Mix in half the egg whites; fold mixture into remaining egg whites.

4. Spoon mixture into lightly greased 1-quart soufflé dish or casserole. Bake at 375 degrees until puffed and golden (sharp knife inserted halfway between center and edges will come out almost clean), 30–35 minutes.

Nutritional Data

PER SERVING		EXCHANGES	
Calories:	358	Milk:	0.0
% Calories from fat:	16	Vegetable:	0.5
Fat (gm):	6.2	Fruit:	0.0
Sat. fat (gm):	1.4	Bread:	1.5
Cholesterol (mg):	2.0	Meat:	1.0
Sodium (mg):	606	Fat:	0.0
Protein (gm):	19.6		
Carbohydrate (gm):	55.4		

MUSHROOM CUSTARD IN ACORN SQUASH

A delicate-textured custard, robustly flavored with portobello mushrooms, is baked in whole acorn squash.

Serves 4

4 small acorn squash (about 1 pound each)
Vegetable cooking spray
8 ounces portobello, *or* cremini, mushrooms, sliced
1 medium onion, chopped
1/2 teaspoon dried rosemary
1/2 teaspoon dried thyme
2 eggs
2 egg whites
1 1/2 cups skim milk
1/2 cup vegetable broth
1/4 teaspoon salt
1/8 teaspoon white pepper

1. Cut small slices from bottoms of squash so they stand upright; cut about 2 inches off stem ends of squash. Scoop out seeds and discard. Stand squash upright in baking pan.

2. Spray medium skillet with vegetable cooking spray; heat over medium heat until hot. Saute mushrooms, onion, rosemary, and thyme until vegetables are tender, about 5 minutes. Cool slightly.

3. Beat eggs and egg whites in medium bowl; beat in milk, broth, salt and pepper. Stir mushroom mixture into custard; then spoon all into squash cavities. Bake, uncovered, at 350 degrees until custard is set and sharp knife inserted into center comes out clean, about 30 minutes.

Nutritional Data

PER SERVING		EXCHANGES	
Calories:	273	Milk:	0.5
% Calories from fat:	17	Vegetable:	1.0
Fat (gm):	5.7	Fruit:	0.0
Sat. fat (gm):	1.2	Bread:	2.5
Cholesterol (mg):	108	Meat:	0.5
Sodium (mg):	270	Fat:	0.5
Protein (gm):	13.8		
Carbohydrate (gm):	50		

EGGS RANCHEROS WITH BLACK BEANS AND 2 SALSAS

------♦------

*Our adaptation of another Mexican favorite,
served with 2 salsas, black beans, and rice.*

Serves 4

Vegetable cooking spray
1¼ cups cholesterol-free egg substitute, *or* 5 eggs
4 corn, *or* flour, tortillas, warm
Fresh Tomato Salsa (recipe follows)
Tomatillo Salsa (recipe follows)
Seasoned Black Beans (recipe follows)
3 cups cooked rice, warm

1. Spray medium skillet with cooking spray; heat over medium heat until hot. Beat egg substitute in small bowl until fluffy; add to skillet and cook over medium-low heat until set, 3–4 minutes, stirring occasionally.

2. Place tortillas on serving plates; spoon scrambled eggs over. Spoon Salsas alongside; serve with Seasoned Black Beans and rice.

Seasoned Black Beans

Makes about 1½ cups

    Vegetable cooking spray
1 medium onion, chopped
2 cloves garlic, minced
1 small jalapeño pepper, minced
1 can (15 ounces) black beans, rinsed, drained
1 cup vegetable broth
½ teaspoon dried cumin
¼ cup finely chopped cilantro leaves

1. Spray medium skillet with cooking spray; heat over medium heat until hot. Saute onion, garlic, and jalapeño pepper until tender, 3–4 minutes. Add beans and broth; cook over medium heat, coarsely mashing beans with fork. Stir in cumin and cilantro.

Fresh Tomato Salsa

Makes about 1 cup

1 large tomato, coarsely chopped
1 small green bell pepper, chopped
1 medium green onion and top, thinly sliced
1 clove garlic, minced
¼–½ teaspoon minced jalapeño pepper
1 tablespoon finely chopped cilantro leaves
¼ teaspoon salt (optional)

1. Combine all ingredients.

Tomatillo Salsa

Makes about 1 cup

8 ounces tomatillos, husks removed
½ small onion, finely chopped
1 clove garlic, minced
¼–½ teaspoon minced jalapeño pepper
1 tablespoon finely chopped cilantro leaves
¼ teaspoon salt (optional)
2–3 pinches sugar

1. Heat tomatillos in 2 inches boiling water in medium saucepan. Reduce heat and simmer, covered, until tomatillos are soft, about 5 minutes. Remove tomatillos from pan and cool; reserve ⅓–½ cup cooking water.

2. Process tomatillos in food processor or blender until coarsely chopped, using pulse technique. Add remaining ingredients; process 1–2 seconds to combine. Stir in reserved cooking water to achieve desired consistency.

Nutritional Data

PER SERVING		EXCHANGES	
Calories:	401	Milk:	0.0
% Calories from fat:	6	Vegetable:	1.5
Fat (gm):	2.8	Fruit:	0.0
Sat. fat (gm):	0.2	Bread:	4.5
Cholesterol (mg):	0	Meat:	1.0
Sodium (mg):	529	Fat:	0.0
Protein (gm):	22.05		
Carbohydrate (gm):	79.5		

BREAKFAST BURRITOS

Not to be limited to breakfast, these chunky burritos are perfect for brunch, lunch, or supper.

Serves 6 (1 burrito each)

Vegetable cooking spray
3 cups cooked, cubed, unpeeled Idaho potatoes
1 cup chopped red, *or* green, bell pepper
1 cup chopped green onion and tops
4 cloves garlic, minced
1½ cups cubed zucchini
¼ cup whole-kernel corn
6 eggs
4 egg whites, *or* ½ cup cholesterol-free egg substitute
¼ cup finely chopped cilantro leaves
¾ teaspoon dried oregano
Salt and pepper, to taste
6 flour tortillas (10-inch)
1 cup (4 ounces) shredded reduced-fat mozzarella, *or* Cheddar, cheese
Cilantro, *or* parsley sprigs, as garnish
1½ cups mild, *or* hot, salsa

1. Spray large skillet with cooking spray; heat over medium heat until hot. Add potatoes, bell pepper, green onions, and garlic; cook over medium heat until potatoes are browned and pepper and onion are tender, about 10 minutes. Add zucchini and corn; cook, covered, until zucchini is tender, about 5 minutes.

2. Beat eggs and egg whites; add eggs, chopped cilantro, and oregano to skillet and cook until eggs are set, stirring occasionally. Season to taste with salt and pepper.

3. Spoon mixture onto tortillas; sprinkle each with equal amount of cheese. Fold 2 sides of each tortilla in about 2 inches, then roll up from other side to enclose filling. Garnish with cilantro sprigs; serve with salsa.

Nutritional Data

PER SERVING		EXCHANGES	
Calories:	441	Milk:	0.0
% Calories from fat:	24	Vegetable:	1.5
Fat (gm):	11.6	Fruit:	0.0
Sat. fat (gm):	4.2	Bread:	3.5
Cholesterol (mg):	223.1	Meat:	2.0
Sodium (mg):	926	Fat:	1.0
Protein (gm):	22.2		
Carbohydrate (gm):	61		

VEGETABLE FRITTATA WITH PARMESAN TOAST

An Italian-style vegetable omelet that is quick and easy to prepare, delicious to eat!

Serves 4

Vegetable cooking spray
1 medium poblano pepper, sliced
1 medium onion, sliced
2 cups mushrooms, sliced
2 cloves garlic, minced
2 tablespoons finely chopped lovage, *or* parsley, leaves
1/4 cup vegetable broth
1 1/2 cups cholesterol-free egg substitute, *or* 6 eggs
1/4 cup skim milk
1/2 cup cooked brown rice
1/2 cup shredded fat-free Cheddar cheese
1/4 teaspoon salt
1/8 teaspoon pepper
4 slices Italian, *or* French, bread
4 teaspoons grated Parmesan cheese

1. Spray medium ovenproof skillet with cooking spray; heat over medium heat until hot. Saute vegetables 5 minutes; add lovage and broth. Cook, covered, over medium heat until vegetables are tender and liquid is absorbed, about 5 minutes.

2. Beat together egg substitute and milk; mix in cooked rice, Cheddar cheese, salt, and pepper. Pour mixture over vegetables in skillet; cook without stirring, uncovered, over medium-low heat until egg is set and lightly browned on bottom, 15–20 minutes.

3. Broil frittata 6 inches from heat source until frittata is cooked on top, 3–4 minutes; invert frittata onto plate, slide back into skillet, and cook until lightly browned, 3–5 minutes.

4. Sprinkle bread with Parmesan cheese; broil 6 inches from heat source until browned, 2–3 minutes. Slide frittata onto serving plate; cut into wedges. Serve with Parmesan toast.

Nutritional Data

PER SERVING		EXCHANGES	
Calories:	212	Milk:	0.0
% Calories from fat:	9	Vegetable:	1.5
Fat (gm):	2.2	Fruit:	0.0
Sat. fat (gm):	0.8	Bread:	1.5
Cholesterol (mg):	4.4	Meat:	1.5
Sodium (mg):	590	Fat:	0.0
Protein (gm):	18.4		
Carbohydrate (gm):	30		

OMELET PUFF WITH VEGETABLE MÉLANGE

Made with beaten egg whites, this oven-baked omelet soars to new heights. Do not overbeat the whites!

Serves 2

    5 egg whites
    ¼ cup water
    ⅓ cup cholesterol-free egg substitute
    ¼ teaspoon dried tarragon
    ¼ teaspoon salt
    ¼ teaspoon pepper
       Vegetable cooking spray
       Vegetable Mélange (recipe follows)
    2 slices crusty Italian bread, warm

1. Beat egg whites in large bowl until foamy; mix in water at high speed, beating until stiff but not dry peaks form. Beat egg substitute, tarragon, salt, and pepper at high speed in small bowl until thick and lemon colored. Fold egg white mixture into egg substitute mixture.

2. Spray 10-inch ovenproof skillet with cooking spray; heat over medium heat until hot. Pour egg mixture into skillet; cook over medium to medium-low heat until bottom of omelet is light brown, about 5 minutes.

3. Bake at 325 degrees, uncovered, until omelet is puffed and light brown. Loosen edge of omelet with spatula; slide onto serving platter, carefully folding omelet in half. Spoon Vegetable Mélange over omelet. Serve with bread.

Vegetable Mélange

Makes about 3 cups

Vegetable cooking spray
2 medium zucchini, sliced
2 medium onions, sliced
2 medium tomatoes, cut into wedges
4 ounces fresh, or frozen (thawed), whole okra
1 medium green bell pepper, sliced
2 tablespoons vegetable broth, *or* water

1. Spray large skillet with cooking spray; heat over medium heat until hot. Saute vegetables until crisp-tender, 3–5 minutes. Add broth; cook, covered, over medium-low heat 5 minutes.

Nutritional Data

PER SERVING		EXCHANGES	
Calories:	264	Milk:	0.0
% Calories from fat:	7	Vegetable:	4.0
Fat (gm):	2.1	Fruit:	0.0
Sat. fat (gm):	0.4	Bread:	1.5
Cholesterol (mg):	0	Meat:	1.5
Sodium (mg):	662	Fat:	0.0
Protein (gm):	20.5		
Carbohydrate (gm):	43.9		

ONION QUICHE

Serves 8

Crust

1½ cups plus 1 tablespoon flour
½ teaspoon baking powder
1/16 teaspoon salt
5 tablespoons canola oil
¼ cup cold water (divided)

Filling

1 tablespoon reduced-calorie margarine
1½ cups (8 ounces) thinly sliced onions
2 tablespoons dry white wine
1 teaspoon sugar
2 ounces reduced-calorie Colby, *or* mild
  Cheddar, cheese, thinly sliced
3 large eggs
4 egg whites
1¾ cups evaporated skim milk
1 teaspoon flour
¼ teaspoon salt
½ teaspoon (scant) ground nutmeg
  Large pinch white pepper

1 recipe Baked Tomatoes (see pg. 168)
4 large cold pears, halved, cored, sliced

1. Make crust: Mix flour with baking powder and salt in bowl. Sprinkle oil over flour; sprinkle 2½ tablespoons water over flour. Stir with fork to combine.

2. Sprinkle a few more drops of water onto flour, stirring with fork. Add as little water as possible, but continue adding water, a few drops at a time, until a handful of dough just holds together when you squeeze it but mixture looks crumbly.

3. Overlap 2 sheets of wax paper on counter; flatten dough slightly on paper. Cover with 2 overlapping sheets of wax paper. Roll dough with rolling pin to a rough circle, about 11-inch diameter, using light strokes. Don't worry if circle isn't perfect.

4. Peel off top wax paper. Lift bottom paper and invert into 10-inch pie pan. Carefully remove paper. Ease dough into pan. Cut around edges with sharp knife. Patch dough with scraps, using gentle finger pressure (no water). Press fork tines around edges.

5. Make filling: Preheat oven to 375 degrees. Melt margarine in nonstick skillet over medium heat. Saute onions 5 minutes, stirring often. Add wine and sugar. Simmer until dry, 4–5 minutes.

6. Lay cheese slices on bottom of crust. Sprinkle onion mixture over Colby. Beat eggs and egg whites with milk, flour, salt, nutmeg, and pepper. Spoon over onion mixture.

7. Bake 40–45 minutes until puffy and golden. Accompany each serving with one-half warm Baked Tomato and one-half cold sliced pear.

Nutritional Data

PER SERVING		EXCHANGES	
Calories:	440	Milk:	0.5
% Calories from fat:	30	Vegetable:	0.5
Fat (gm):	15.2	Fruit:	2.0
Sat. fat (gm):	2.7	Bread:	1.5
Cholesterol (mg):	87.3	Meat:	1.0
Sodium (mg):	438	Fat:	2.5
Protein (gm):	15.9		
Carbohydrate (gm):	63.3		

SPINACH, ONION, AND CHEESE QUICHE

This quiche is as good cold as it is warm. Brown-bag a slice of it for lunch—if you have any leftover, that is!

Serves 8

Crust (pg. 114)
2 tablespoons grated Parmesan cheese
3/4 cup chopped onion
1 tablespoon reduced-fat margarine
2 packages (10 ounces each) frozen (thawed) chopped spinach, well drained
1 cup cholesterol-free egg substitute
1 cup evaporated skim milk
3/4 cup skim milk
1 teaspoon flour
1/2 teaspoon ground nutmeg
1/2 teaspoon salt
1/4 teaspoon pepper
4 chilled pears, cored, sliced

1. Roll Crust on lightly floured surface to 11-inch diameter. Ease pastry into 10-inch pie pan; trim and flute edge. Sprinkle Parmesan cheese over bottom of crust.

2. Saute onion in margarine in medium skillet until tender, about 5 minutes. Add spinach; cook over medium heat until mixture is dry, 2–3 minutes. Spoon mixture into crust.

3. Beat egg substitute, evaporated skim milk, skim milk, flour, nutmeg, salt, and pepper until blended; pour over spinach mixture in Crust.

4. Bake at 375 degrees until Crust is brown and quiche is just firm, about 50 minutes. Cool 10 minutes before serving. Accompany each serving with half a sliced pear.

Nutritional Data

PER SERVING		EXCHANGES	
Calories:	305	Milk:	0.5
% Calories from fat:	30	Vegetable:	1.0
Fat (gm):	10.6	Fruit:	0.5
Sat. fat (gm):	1.2	Bread:	1.5
Cholesterol (mg):	3	Meat:	1.0
Sodium (mg):	374	Fat:	2.0
Protein (gm):	12		
Carbohydrate (gm):	42.3		

EGG AND CHEESE CASSEROLE

Serves 4

Vegetable cooking spray
1/2 cup egg substitute, *or* 2 eggs
2 large eggs
4 large egg whites
1 1/2 cups evaporated skim milk
1 teaspoon sugar
1 teaspoon baking powder
1/4 teaspoon salt (optional)
Pinch cayenne
Pinch ground nutmeg
1 cup 1% cottage cheese
2 tablespoons fat-free sour cream
2 tablespoons flour
2 ounces reduced-calorie sharp Cheddar cheese, grated

1. Preheat oven to 325 degrees. Spray 10 x 8-inch casserole with cooking spray.

2. In electric mixing bowl, beat egg substitute, eggs, and egg whites with milk, sugar, baking powder, (optional) salt, cayenne, and nutmeg until combined. Add cottage cheese and sour cream and mix well. Beat in flour.

3. Stir Cheddar into mixture. Spoon into prepared casserole. Bake 40–45 minutes or until puffy.

Nutritional Data

PER SERVING			EXCHANGES	
Calories:	242		Milk:	1.0
% Calories from fat:	20		Vegetable:	0.0
Fat (gm):	5.3		Fruit:	0.0
Sat. fat (gm):	2.3		Bread:	0.5
Cholesterol (mg):	120		Meat:	2.5
Sodium (mg):	748		Fat:	0.0
Protein (gm):	27.4			
Carbohydrate (gm):	19.5			

9
SANDWICHES

Herbed Veggie Burgers

Soybean-Veggie Burgers

Spicy Black Bean and Corn Pockets

French Bread Stuffed with Vegetable Pâté

Sandwich Roll with Cream Cheese and Olives

Vegetable Hero with Tofu Aioli

Roasted Rutabaga and Eggplant Sandwich
with Rémoulade Sauce

HERBED VEGGIE BURGERS

*Serve also as an entree, accompanied with Baked Tomatoes
and Sweet Potato Pone (see pgs. 168, 105).*

Serves 4

Vegetable cooking spray
3/4 cup finely chopped broccoflower florets
3/4 cup finely chopped mushrooms
1/4 cup finely chopped onion
2 cloves garlic
1½ teaspoons dried basil (divided)
1/2 teaspoon dried marjoram
1/4 teaspoon dried thyme
2/3 cup cooked wild, *or* brown, rice
1/3 cup quick-cooking oats
1/3 cup coarsely chopped toasted walnuts
1/2 cup 1% fat cottage cheese
1/2 cup fat-free Cheddar cheese
Salt and pepper, to taste
2 egg whites
1/2 cup fat-free mayonnaise
4 multigrain, *or* whole wheat, buns, toasted
Lettuce leaves, as garnish

1. Spray medium skillet with cooking spray; heat over medium heat until hot. Saute broccoflower, mushrooms, onion, and garlic until tender, 8–10 minutes. Add ½ teaspoon basil, marjoram, and thyme and cook 1–2 minutes longer. Remove from heat and cool slightly.

2. Stir rice, oats, walnuts, and cheeses into vegetable mixture; season to taste with salt and pepper. Stir in egg whites. Form mixture into 4 burgers.

3. Spray large skillet with cooking spray; heat over medium heat until hot. Add burgers and cook over medium to medium-low heat until browned on the bottoms, 3–4 minutes. Spray tops of burgers with cooking spray and turn; cook until browned, 3–4 minutes.

4. Mix mayonnaise and remaining 1 teaspoon basil; spread on bottoms of buns, and top with lettuce, burgers, and bun tops.

Nutritional Data

PER SERVING		EXCHANGES	
Calories:	322	Milk:	0.0
% Calories from fat:	26	Vegetable:	2.0
Fat (gm):	9.5	Fruit:	0.0
Sat. fat (gm):	1.3	Bread:	2.0
Cholesterol (mg):	1.3	Meat:	1.5
Sodium (mg):	828	Fat:	1.7
Protein (gm):	19.7		
Carbohydrate (gm):	42		

SOYBEAN-VEGGIE BURGERS

These burgers pack a hefty nutritional punch and taste as good as they are good for you! Soybeans triple in volume when cooked, so you will need only $1/3$ cup of dried soybeans for this recipe.

Serves 4

Vegetable cooking spray
$1/2$ cup finely chopped onion
$1/2$ cup finely chopped carrot
$1/4$ cup finely chopped red bell pepper
4 cloves garlic, minced
1 cup cooked soybeans, coarsely pureed
1 cup cooked basmati, *or* pecan, rice
$1/2$ cup seasoned dry breadcrumbs
3 tablespoons finely chopped parsley leaves
Red pepper sauce, to taste
Salt and pepper, to taste
1 egg
4 whole wheat buns, toasted
4 teaspoons spicy brown mustard, *or* horseradish mustard
Lettuce leaves, as garnish

1. Spray medium skillet with cooking spray; heat over medium heat until hot. Add onion, carrot, bell pepper, and garlic and saute until tender, about 8 minutes.

2. Combine soybeans, rice, sauteed vegetables, breadcrumbs, and parsley in bowl; season to taste with red pepper sauce, salt, and pepper. Mix in egg, blending well; form mixture into 4 burgers.

3. Spray large skillet with cooking spray; heat over medium heat until hot. Add burgers and cook over medium to medium-low heat until browned on the bottoms, 3–4 minutes. Spray tops of burgers with cooking spray; turn burgers and cook until browned, 3–4 minutes.

4. Spread bottoms of buns with mustard; top with lettuce, burgers, and bun tops.

Nutritional Data

PER SERVING		EXCHANGES	
Calories:	317	Milk:	0.0
% Calories from fat:	20	Vegetable:	1.0
Fat (gm):	7.3	Fruit:	0.0
Sat. fat (gm):	1.3	Bread:	3.0
Cholesterol (mg):	53.3	Meat:	1.0
Sodium (mg):	695	Fat:	0.5
Protein (gm):	16.9		
Carbohydrate (gm):	49.6		

SPICY BLACK BEAN AND CORN POCKETS

It takes just minutes to make this delicious entree, which resembles a chili sandwich.

Serves 8 (1 pocket each)

1 can (15 ounces) black beans
¼ cup chopped canned mild chilies
1 tablespoon reduced-calorie margarine
1 teaspoon minced garlic
1 cup minced red onion (divided)
5 teaspoons chili powder
1 teaspoon dried cumin
½ teaspoon salt (optional)
⅛ teaspoon cayenne
1¼ cups (heaping) frozen corn, thawed
3 tablespoons lime juice (divided)
3 tablespoons water
8 sourdough pita pockets (2 ounces each)

Toppings

½ cup seeded, chopped, drained tomatoes
½ cup peeled, chopped jicama
¼ cup fat-free sour cream
½ cup coarsely chopped cilantro leaves

1. Preheat oven to 350 degrees. Place beans in colander under running tap water until canning liquid is removed; reserve. Place canned chilies in strainer under running tap water for 3 minutes to remove salty canning liquid; reserve.

2. Heat margarine in large nonstick skillet over medium heat. Saute garlic 1 minute. Add ½ cup onion and saute 4 minutes more. Stir in chili powder, cumin, (optional) salt, and cayenne.

3 Add corn, rinsed chilies, 2 tablespoons lime juice, and 3 tablespoons water. Simmer until corn is cooked, liquid has evaporated, and vegetables are coated with spices. Stir in beans, mixing well. Spoon into serving bowl.

4. Meanwhile, cut 1 inch off top of each pita and place on cookie sheet. Place in oven and heat 1 minute or until just warm.

5. Spoon remaining ½ cup minced onion into small bowl. Spoon tomatoes, jicama, sour cream, and cilantro into four separate small bowls. Sprinkle remaining 1 tablespoon lime juice over jicama.

6. Bring bowl of beans/corn mixture, warmed pitas, and toppings to table. Each guest takes 1 pita and spoons about 6 tablespoons of beans/corn mixture into pocket. Each pocket should be topped with 1 tablespoon each onion, tomatoes, and jicama, 1½ teaspoons sour cream, and 1 tablespoon cilantro.

Nutritional Data

PER SERVING		EXCHANGES	
Calories:	245	Milk:	0.0
% Calories from fat:	4	Vegetable:	0.5
Fat (gm):	2.3	Fruit:	0.0
Sat. fat (gm):	0.3	Bread:	3.0
Cholesterol (mg):	0	Meat:	0.0
Sodium (mg):	384	Fat:	0.5
Protein (gm):	11.5		
Carbohydrate (gm):	49		

FRENCH BREAD STUFFED WITH VEGETABLE PÂTÉ

This sandwich is made with French bread that's hollowed out, then stuffed with vegetable pâté and baked. It can be served warm or cold.

Serves 4

- 1 tablespoon reduced-calorie margarine
- 1 teaspoon minced garlic
- 1/3 cup finely minced red onion
- 3 green onions, green parts only, minced
- 1 slice reduced-calorie white bread
- 2 cups frozen baby lima beans, thawed
- 1/2 cup egg substitute, *or* 2 eggs
- 2 tablespoons skim milk
- 1/2 teaspoon salt
  Large pinch cayenne
- 1 cup frozen corn kernels, thawed
- 1/3 cup chopped cilantro leaves
- 3/4 cup peeled, grated carrots
- 1 loaf French bread, 16-inch
- 8 sprigs cilantro

1. Preheat oven to 350 degrees. Melt margarine in nonstick skillet over medium-low heat. Saute garlic 1 minute. Raise heat to medium and add red and green onions. Saute 5 minutes more. Reserve.

2. Quarter white bread and place in food processor or blender and make crumbs.

3. Place limas in food processor with egg substitute, milk, salt, and cayenne. Process until coarsely pureed. Spoon into bowl. Add onion mixture, corn, cilantro, carrots, and breadcrumbs. Mix very well.

4. Slice both ends off a 16-inch French bread. Use serrated bread knife to hollow out center, working slowly and carefully to remove white bread without making holes in crust. Stand bread on one end and carefully pack filling into bread.

5. Wrap bread tightly in foil and place in oven. Bake 30 minutes. Remove from oven, remove foil, and allow to cool slightly. Use serrated knife to cut loaf into 4 sections, each about 3½ inches long. Garnish each sandwich with 2 cilantro sprigs.

Nutritional Data

PER SERVING		EXCHANGES	
Calories:	187	Milk:	0.0
% Calories from fat:	9	Vegetable:	0.5
Fat (gm):	2	Fruit:	0.0
Sat. fat (gm):	0.4	Bread:	2.0
Cholesterol (mg):	0.1	Meat:	0.5
Sodium (mg):	410	Fat:	0.0
Protein (gm):	11.4		
Carbohydrate (gm):	33.1		

SANDWICH ROLL WITH CREAM CHEESE AND OLIVES

This unusual sandwich is made with a thin, flat, round (about 16-inch diameter) of Armenian-style cracker bread called Hye Roller. The bread, which comes in packages of three, is meant to be spread with sandwich fillings, rolled up, and sliced. Or you can use a Lebanese lahvosh. This thin, flat, oval bread (about 22 x 15 inches) can also be filled and rolled if you first wrap it in a damp kitchen towel until it softens. If neither bread is easily available, write to Hye Quality Bakery, 2222 Santa Clara, Fresno, CA 92721, (209) 455-1511, and ask where Hye Roller is sold in your area.

Serves 4

- 2 Hye Rollers, *or* lahvosh
- 10 ounces fat-free cream cheese (not tub type), room temperature
- 1/2 cup minced green onion, green part only
- 1/2 cup chopped cilantro leaves
- 16 large, pitted, kalamata olives, or other brined olives, chopped (about 1/2 cup)
- 20 spinach leaves, stems removed, washed and well dried
- 2 firm tomatoes (about 10 ounces each), cut in ultra-thin slices

1. Place flat breads on counter. Trim each with scissors to about 15 x 16 inches or you will not have enough filling.

2. Spread breads with cream cheese, smoothing it out to the far edges. Sprinkle rolls with scallions, cilantro, and olives, leaving a 4-inch section empty of everything but cream cheese at one end.

3. Arrange spinach leaves in single layer over scallions. Pat tomato slices dry with paper towels. Arrange them over spinach leaves.

4. Roll bread as tightly as possible. Press the "empty" end sections to rolls, so the cheese adheres. Wrap sandwiches tightly in plastic wrap or foil. Store in refrigerator until serving time, no more than a couple of hours. Cut each roll in half for 4 servings.

Nutritional Data

PER SERVING		EXCHANGES	
Calories:	144	Milk:	0.0
% Calories from fat:	23	Vegetable:	1.5
Fat (gm):	3.6	Fruit:	0.0
Sat. fat (gm):	0.2	Bread:	0.5
Cholesterol (mg):	12.5	Meat:	1.5
Sodium (mg):	781	Fat:	0.0
Protein (gm):	13.3		
Carbohydrate (gm):	14		

VEGETABLE HERO WITH TOFU AIOLI

Serves 4

Tofu Aioli Sauce

1 cup soft tofu
2 tablespoons canola oil
1 teaspoon white wine vinegar
1 teaspoon lemon juice
1/4 teaspoon salt (optional)
1/4 teaspoon dried turmeric
1/4 teaspoon dry mustard
   Large pinch white pepper
6 garlic cloves, peeled, coarsely chopped

Sandwich

  2 tablespoons reduced-calorie margarine, melted
1/3 cup lemon juice
  1 teaspoon dried thyme
1/2 teaspoon garlic powder
1/2 teaspoon onion powder
1/4 teaspoon salt (optional)
  8 ounces portobello mushrooms, sliced 1/2 inch
    thick, lengthwise through caps and stems
  1 16-inch loaf French bread
1/4 cup chopped cilantro leaves
  6 curly lettuce leaves, washed and dried
  1 firm tomato, thinly sliced

1. Make tofu aioli: Place tofu, oil, vinegar, lemon juice, (optional) salt, turmeric, mustard, and pepper in food processor. Pulse to combine. Add garlic and pulse until incorporated.

2. Make Sandwich: Melt margarine in small saucepan and stir in lemon juice, thyme, garlic powder, onion powder, and (optional) salt. Place mushrooms in plastic bag. Scrape mixture into bag with mushrooms and toss bag lightly to coat.

3. Remove mushrooms from bag and discard marinade. Heat a nonstick skillet over high heat. Add mushroom slices, a few at a time, and saute them until lightly brown on each side.

4. Halve loaf lengthwise. Remove some bread down the center of top half so it resembles a water trough. Toast both halves lightly under broiler. Spread both halves with Tofu Aioli.

5. Sprinkle cilantro over aioli on bottom half. Arrange lettuce in overlapping fashion on cilantro. Overlap tomato slices on lettuce. Place mushrooms in trough of top half. Press the two loaf halves together firmly. Cut into quarters.

Nutritional Data

PER SERVING		EXCHANGES	
Calories:	476	Milk:	0.0
% Calories from fat:	30	Vegetable:	1.0
Fat (gm):	16.4	Fruit:	0.0
Sat. fat (gm):	2	Bread:	4.0
Cholesterol (mg):	0	Meat:	0.5
Sodium (mg):	769	Fat:	3.0
Protein (gm):	16		
Carbohydrate (gm):	68.5		

ROASTED RUTABAGA AND EGGPLANT SANDWICH WITH RÉMOULADE SAUCE

*This sandwich includes a delicious tofu-based rémoulade sauce
that requires no cooking but adds a very special flavor.*

Serves 8

1 cup buttermilk
¼ cup egg substitute
1 teaspoon Tabasco sauce
2 cups fine breadcrumbs, made in blender or
food processor from reduced-calorie bread
(about 6 slices)
¼ teaspoon salt
⅛ teaspoon white pepper
8 large, round rutabaga slices, peeled, each
⅓ inch thick
8 large round eggplant slices, each ⅓ inch thick
8 4-inch bakery-quality kaiser, *or* butterflake,
rolls, split for sandwiches
16 leaves curly lettuce, red or green
8 slices large, firm tomato
Rémoulade Sauce (recipe follows)

1. Preheat oven to 400 degrees. Line cookie sheet with baking parchment. Combine buttermilk, egg substitute, and Tabasco sauce in large plastic bag. Mix crumbs with salt and pepper and distribute in flat baking pan.

2. Place rutabaga and eggplant slices in plastic bag with buttermilk mixture and let stand 15 minutes, turning occasionally. Remove slices one by one and press both sides into crumbs. Place coated slices on lined cookie sheet.

3. Bake 15 minutes, turn vegetables, and bake another 5 minutes. Remove eggplant and allow to cool. Continue baking rutabaga another 20–25 minutes or until soft.

4. While vegetables bake, make sauce. Assemble sandwiches as follows: Spread 1 tablespoon sauce on each half of roll. Place 1 lettuce leaf on

bottom half of roll. Add 1 slice rutabaga, 1 slice tomato, 1 slice egg-plant, and 1 lettuce leaf, before closing sandwich with top half of roll. Serve immediately.

Rémoulade Sauce

- 1 cup soft tofu
- 3 tablespoons canola oil
- 2 teaspoons lemon juice
- 1/4 teaspoon salt
- 1/4 teaspoon dried turmeric
- 1/4 teaspoon dry mustard
- 1/8 teaspoon cayenne
- 1/8 teaspoon white pepper
- 2 tablespoons minced parsley leaves
- 1 tablespoon sweet pickle relish
- 2 teaspoons minced green onion, green part only
- 2 teaspoons small capers, pressed in strainer to extract liquid

1. Place tofu, oil, lemon juice, salt, turmeric, dry mustard, cayenne, and white pepper in food processor or blender container. Process until well mixed. Spoon into bowl. Stir in parsley, relish, scallions, and capers.

Nutritional Data

PER SERVING		EXCHANGES	
Calories:	375	Milk:	0.0
% Calories from fat:	25	Vegetable:	3.0
Fat (gm):	10.4	Fruit:	0.0
Sat. fat (gm):	1.4	Bread:	3.0
Cholesterol (mg):	1.1	Meat:	0.0
Sodium (mg):	775	Fat:	2.0
Protein (gm):	13.2		
Carbohydrate (gm):	57.1		

10
SALADS

Vegetable Salad with Millet

Broccoli Salad with Sour Cream-Mayonnaise Dressing

12-Layer Salad

Garden Pasta Salad with Crostini

Oriental Noodle Salad

Tabbouleh and Vegetable Salad Medley

Vegetable Salad with 2 Beans

Black Beans and Rice Salad

Russian Salad

VEGETABLE SALAD WITH MILLET

Finely chop the vegetables by hand or in a food processor.
Serve this salad in bowls, in beefsteak tomato halves,
or use it as a filling for warm pita pockets.

Serves 6 (about 1⅓ cups each)

1¼ cups millet
3⅓ cups water
½ cup sliced celery
½ medium red bell pepper, sliced
4 green onions, green and white parts, sliced
1 medium carrot, sliced
¼ cup finely chopped parsley leaves
2 tablespoons finely chopped fresh basil leaves,
   or 1 teaspoon dried basil
½ head iceberg lettuce, sliced
½ head green leaf lettuce, sliced
1 medium tomato, coarsely chopped
   Oregano Vinaigrette (recipe follows)
   Salt, to taste
   Pepper, to taste
   Spinach, *or* lettuce, leaves, as garnish
4 pita pockets

1. Cook millet in large saucepan over medium heat until toasted, 2–3 minutes. Add water and heat to boiling; reduce heat and simmer, covered, until millet is tender and liquid absorbed, about 15 minutes. Remove from heat and let stand, covered, 10 minutes. Cool to room temperature.

2. Combine celery, bell pepper, green onions, carrot, parsley, and basil in food processor; process, using pulse technique, until finely chopped. Transfer mixture to large bowl.

3. Add lettuce to food processor; process, using pulse technique, until finely chopped. Transfer mixture to bowl with vegetables.

4. Add tomatoes and millet to vegetable mixture and toss; drizzle with Oregano Vinaigrette and toss. Season to taste with salt and pepper. Spoon salad into spinach-lined salad bowls; serve with pita pockets.

Oregano Vinaigrette

Makes about ⅓ cup

3 tablespoons olive oil, *or* vegetable oil
3 tablespoons white wine vinegar
1 teaspoon dried oregano

1. Mix all ingredients; refrigerate until ready to serve.

Nutritional Data

PER SERVING		EXCHANGES	
Calories:	383	Milk:	0.0
% Calories from fat:	23	Vegetable:	1.0
Fat (gm):	9.6	Fruit:	0.0
Sat. fat (gm):	1.4	Bread:	4.0
Cholesterol (mg):	0	Meat:	0.0
Sodium (mg):	238	Fat:	1.5
Protein (gm):	10.3		
Carbohydrate (gm):	63.9		

BROCCOLI SALAD WITH SOUR CREAM-MAYONNAISE DRESSING

◆

Serve this hearty salad on a bed of salad greens, spinach, thinly sliced red cabbage, or in scooped out tomato halves. The blue cheese can be deleted from the dressing, if desired.

Serves 4

4½ cups sliced broccoli florets and celery stalks
1½ cups sliced zucchini
1½ cups chopped green bell peppers
1½ cups sliced mushrooms
12 cherry tomatoes, cut into halves
3 green onions, green and white parts, sliced
2 tablespoons dark raisins
   Sour Cream-Mayonnaise Dressing
   (recipe follows)
   Leaf lettuce, as garnish

1. Combine all ingredients in salad bowl; toss with dressing. Serve in lettuce-lined salad bowls.

Sour Cream-Mayonnaise Dressing

Makes about 1 1/4 cups

- 1/3 cup fat-free sour cream
- 1/3 cup fat-free mayonnaise
- 3 cloves garlic, minced
- 3 tablespoons skim milk
- 3 tablespoons crumbled blue cheese

1. Mix all ingredients.

Nutritional Data

PER SERVING		EXCHANGES	
Calories:	152	Milk:	0.0
% Calories from fat:	15	Vegetable:	4.0
Fat (gm):	2.8	Fruit:	0.0
Sat. fat (gm):	1.3	Bread:	0.5
Cholesterol (mg):	5	Meat:	0.0
Sodium (mg):	399	Fat:	0.5
Protein (gm):	8.8		
Carbohydrate (gm):	28		

12-LAYER SALAD

A new look at an old favorite! This attractive salad is conveniently assembled, topped with dressing, refrigerated up to a day in advance, and then tossed before serving.

Serves 6

    2 cups sliced spinach leaves
    2 medium carrots
1½ cups sliced celery
    2 cups thinly sliced red cabbage
    2 cups small broccoli florets
    2 cups chopped iceberg lettuce
    1 medium yellow bell pepper, sliced
    1 medium tomato, sliced
1½ cups cut green beans, cooked until crisp-
       tender, cooled
    1 cup finely chopped parsley (divided)
    1 can (15 ounces) dark red kidney beans, rinsed,
       drained
    1 medium red onion, thinly sliced
       Garlic Dressing (recipe follows)
    3 hard-boiled eggs, cut into wedges

1. Layer spinach, carrots, celery, cabbage, broccoli, lettuce, peppers, tomatoes, green beans, ½ cup parsley, kidney beans, and onion in 2½-quart glass salad bowl. Spread dressing over top and sprinkle with remaining ½ cup parsley. Refrigerate up to 24 hours.

2. Before serving, toss salad and place egg wedges on top.

Garlic Dressing

Makes about 1½ cups

¾ cup fat-free mayonnaise, *or* salad dressing
¾ cup fat-free sour cream
    4 cloves garlic, minced
    1 teaspoon dried basil
    1 teaspoon dried oregano
¾ teaspoon dried tarragon

1. Combine all ingredients; refrigerate until ready to use.

Nutritional Data

PER SERVING		EXCHANGES	
Calories:	214	Milk:	0.0
% Calories from fat:	14	Vegetable:	3.0
Fat (gm):	3.7	Fruit:	0.0
Sat. fat (gm):	0.9	Bread:	1.0
Cholesterol (mg):	106.5	Meat:	1.0
Sodium (mg):	637	Fat:	0.0
Protein (gm):	14.8		
Carbohydrate (gm):	37.8		

GARDEN PASTA SALAD WITH CROSTINI

Serve this salad warm, or refrigerate it for several hours and serve cold. Any shaped pasta can be substituted for the shells; breadsticks can be substituted for the crostini.

Serves 4 (about 1²/₃ cups each)

Olive oil cooking spray
3 cups broccoli florets
2 cups cut asparagus (1-inch pieces)
1 medium yellow bell pepper, cut in 1-inch slices
3 green onions, green and white parts, sliced
¼ cup chopped red onion
½ cup frozen whole kernel corn, thawed
1 clove garlic, minced
1½ cups small pasta shells, cooked *al dente*, warm
1 can (15 ounces) dark red kidney beans, rinsed, drained
1½ cups halved cherry tomatoes
3 tablespoons finely chopped fresh, *or* 1½ teaspoons dried, basil
1½ tablespoons olive oil, *or* vegetable oil
1½ tablespoons red wine vinegar
2 tablespoons crumbled feta cheese
4 slices Italian bread
1 clove garlic, cut in half

1. Spray large skillet with cooking spray; heat over medium heat until hot. Saute broccoli, asparagus, bell pepper, green and red onions, corn, and garlic until crisp-tender, about 5 minutes. Toss with warm pasta, beans, tomatoes, and basil in salad bowl.

2. Combine oil and vinegar; drizzle over salad and toss. Sprinkle with cheese.

3. Rub both sides of bread with cut clove of garlic; broil 4 inches from heat source until golden on both sides.

Nutritional Data

PER SERVING		EXCHANGES	
Calories:	470	Milk:	0.0
% Calories from fat:	18	Vegetable:	3.0
Fat (gm):	10	Fruit:	0.0
Sat. fat (gm):	2.3	Bread:	4.5
Cholesterol (mg):	7.1	Meat:	0.5
Sodium (mg):	496	Fat:	1.0
Protein (gm):	22.7		
Carbohydrate (gm):	82.5		

ORIENTAL NOODLE SALAD

Use dark oriental sesame oil for the fullest flavor; the light oil is much more subtle in taste.

Serves 4 (about 2 cups each)

1 package (3 ounces) ramen noodles
1 cup trimmed snow peas, steamed until crisp-tender
1 cup halved Brussels sprouts, steamed until crisp-tender
1 medium red bell pepper, sliced
1 cup sliced mushrooms
1 cup bean sprouts
2 medium carrots, thinly sliced
1/2 cup frozen peas, thawed
1 can (11 ounces) Mandarin orange segments, drained
1/4 cup finely chopped parsley
1/3 cup orange juice
1 tablespoon sesame oil

2 cloves garlic, minced
$1/2$ teaspoon five-spice powder
$1/4$ teaspoon salt
$1/4$ teaspoon white pepper
2 teaspoons toasted sesame seeds (optional)

1. Lightly break noodles apart and cook according to package directions, but do not use spice packet; cool.

2. Combine noodles, vegetables, orange segments, and parsley in large bowl; toss.

3. Combine in small bowl, remaining ingredients, except sesame seeds; pour over salad and toss. Spoon salad onto plates; sprinkle with sesame seeds if desired.

Nutritional Data

PER SERVING		EXCHANGES	
Calories:	252	Milk:	0.0
% Calories from fat:	25	Vegetable:	3.5
Fat (gm):	7.5	Fruit:	0.5
Sat. fat (gm):	0.8	Bread:	1.0
Cholesterol (mg):	13.3	Meat:	0.0
Sodium (mg):	497	Fat:	1.5
Protein (gm):	9.2		
Carbohydrate (gm):	41.6		

TABBOULEH AND VEGETABLE SALAD MEDLEY

Two salads—a tabbouleh salad dressed with Lemon-Cinnamon Vinaigrette; and a mixed vegetables salad with chunky Cucumber-Sour Cream Dressing—are lightly combined for a contrast of flavors. If desired, the salads can be arranged side by side on serving plates.

Serves 4

1 package (5¼ ounces) tabbouleh wheat salad mix
1 cup cold water
½ cup finely chopped celery
⅓ cup sliced green onion, green and white parts
8 prunes, pitted, chopped
2 tablespoons finely chopped parsley
1 tablespoon finely chopped fresh, *or* 1 teaspoon dried basil
1 clove garlic, minced
Lemon-Cinnamon Vinaigrette (recipe follows)
Salt, to taste
Pepper, to taste
2 cups cauliflower florets
¾ cup coarsely chopped red bell pepper
2 medium carrots, diagonally sliced
8 cherry tomatoes, halved
Cucumber-Sour Cream Dressing (recipe follows)
Salad greens, as garnish
2 tablespoons feta cheese (optional)

1. Mix tabbouleh and cold water in small bowl, discarding spice packet; let stand 30 minutes. Stir celery, green onion, prunes, parsley, basil, and garlic into tabbouleh; add Lemon-Cinnamon Vinaigrette and toss. Season to taste with salt and pepper.

2. Combine cauliflower, bell pepper, carrots, and tomatoes; spoon Cucumber-Sour Cream Dressing over and toss. Season to taste with salt and pepper.

3. Gently toss vegetable salad into tabbouleh salad. Spoon medley into lettuce-lined serving bowls. Sprinkle with feta cheese.

Lemon-Cinnamon Vinaigrette

Makes about ¹/₂ cup

¹/₃ cup lemon juice

3 tablespoons olive oil, *or* vegetable oil

¹/₄ teaspoon dried cinnamon

1. Combine all ingredients; refrigerate until ready to serve.

Cucumber-Sour Cream Dressing

Makes about 1 cup

¹/₂ cup fat-free sour cream

¹/₄ cup fat-free plain yogurt

1 teaspoon white wine vinegar

1 teaspoon dried dill weed

¹/₂ medium cucumber, peeled, seeded, chopped

1. Combine all ingredients; refrigerate until ready to serve.

Nutritional Data

PER SERVING		EXCHANGES	
Calories:	301	Milk:	0.0
% Calories from fat:	30	Vegetable:	3.5
Fat (gm):	11	Fruit:	1.5
Sat. fat (gm):	1.5	Bread:	0.5
Cholesterol (mg):	0.3	Meat:	0.0
Sodium (mg):	250	Fat:	2.0
Protein (gm):	7.9		
Carbohydrate (gm):	48.7		

VEGETABLE SALAD WITH 2 BEANS

Enjoy the fresh flavors of cilantro and orange and the accent of jalapeño pepper in this mixed vegetable salad.

Serves 4 (about 1½ cups each)

1 pound cooked Idaho potatoes, unpeeled, cut in
    1-inch cubes, cooled
½ pound cooked baby lima beans, cooled
1 can (15 ounces) garbanzo beans, rinsed,
    drained
1 medium cucumber, peeled, seeded, chopped
1 medium zucchini, sliced
1 small green bell pepper, chopped
¼ cup chopped cilantro leaves
    Orange Vinaigrette (recipe follows)
    Salt, to taste
    Pepper, to taste
    Salad greens, as garnish

1. Combine vegetables and cilantro in salad bowl and toss. Drizzle dressing over salad and toss; season to taste with salt and pepper. Spoon salad over greens on salad plates.

Orange Vinaigrette

Makes about ⅔ cup

¼ cup fresh orange juice
¼ cup fresh lime juice
2 tablespoons olive oil, *or* vegetable oil
1 teaspoon dried cumin
1 teaspoon minced jalapeño pepper
½ teaspoon paprika
¼ teaspoon cayenne

1. Mix all ingredients; refrigerate until ready to serve.

Nutritional Data

PER SERVING		EXCHANGES	
Calories:	480	Milk:	0.0
% Calories from fat:	17	Vegetable:	1.0
Fat (gm):	9.6	Fruit:	0.0
Sat. fat (gm):	1.3	Bread:	5.0
Cholesterol (mg):	0	Meat:	0.0
Sodium (mg):	477	Fat:	2.0
Protein (gm):	18.4		
Carbohydrate (gm):	83.7		

BLACK BEANS AND RICE SALAD

*Apple adds a fresh flavor accent to this colorful salad;
use your favorite variety: sweet or tart.*

Serves 4 (about 2 cups each)

1 cup cooked rice, cooled
1 can (15 ounces) black beans, rinsed, drained
1½ cups sliced bok choy (Chinese cabbage)
1½ cups thinly sliced red cabbage
1 cup cubed cucumber, peeled, seeded
2 green onions, green and white parts, sliced
2 tablespoons thinly sliced celery
1 medium apple, cored, cubed
2 tablespoons dark raisins
¼ cup finely chopped cilantro leaves
3 tablespoons balsamic vinegar
3 tablespoons olive oil, *or* vegetable oil
1½ teaspoons Dijon-style mustard
Salt, to taste
Pepper, to taste

1. Combine rice, beans, vegetables, apple, raisins, and cilantro in large bowl; toss. Combine vinegar, oil, and mustard; drizzle over salad and toss. Season to taste with salt and pepper

Nutritional Data

PER SERVING		EXCHANGES	
Calories:	409	Milk:	0.0
% Calories from fat:	24	Vegetable:	0.0
Fat (gm):	11.9	Fruit:	0.5
Sat. fat (gm):	1.5	Bread:	4.0
Cholesterol (mg):	0	Meat:	0.0
Sodium (mg):	376	Fat:	2.0
Protein (gm):	13.6		
Carbohydrate (gm):	69.8		

RUSSIAN SALAD

Classically, Russian salad consists of cubes of assorted vegetables tossed with a seasoned mayonnaise mixed with dill pickle, capers, parsley, and chives or scallions. Our version includes veggies and seasonings but substitutes a low-fat tofu-based Russian Dressing sparked with chopped dill pickle, green onion, and capers.

Serves 4 (about 2 cups each)

2 cups peeled, cubed potatoes, cooked
1 cup frozen baby carrots, cooked, cut into thirds
1 cup frozen peas, cooked
1 cup frozen cut green beans, cooked
1 cup frozen baby lima beans, cooked
1 cup canned julienne-style beets, rinsed well, drained
1 cup canned artichoke hearts, rinsed, drained, cut into eighths
1/2 cup chopped fresh parsley leaves
Russian Dressing (recipe follows)

1. Combine vegetables in salad bowl; spoon Russian Dressing over and toss. Spoon onto plates and sprinkle with parsley.

Russian Dressing

Makes about 2¼ cups

1 cup soft tofu, drained
3 tablespoons canola oil

$\frac{1}{4}$ cup water

2 teaspoons white wine vinegar

$\frac{1}{2}$ teaspoon salt

$\frac{1}{4}$ teaspoon dried turmeric

$\frac{1}{4}$ teaspoon dry mustard

$\frac{1}{8}$ teaspoon cayenne

$\frac{1}{2}$ cup fat-free sour cream

$\frac{1}{2}$ cup finely chopped parsley leaves

2 tablespoons finely chopped dill pickle

2 tablespoons finely chopped green onion tops

2 teaspoons drained capers

1. Process tofu, oil, water, vinegar, salt, turmeric, mustard, and cayenne pepper in food processor or blender until smooth. Stir in remaining ingredients. Refrigerate until ready to use.

Nutritional Data

PER SERVING		EXCHANGES	
Calories:	395	Milk:	0.0
% Calories from fat:	30	Vegetable:	3.0
Fat (gm):	13.9	Fruit:	0.0
Sat. fat (gm):	1.3	Bread:	2.5
Cholesterol (mg):	0	Meat:	1.0
Sodium (mg):	755	Fat:	2.0
Protein (gm):	17.2		
Carbohydrate (gm):	56.2		

11
ETHNIC SPECIALTIES

Colombian Style Vegetable Plate with Spicy Tomato Sauce

Normandy Vegetables with Normandy Sauce

Irish Colcannon

Italian Caponata on Cabbage

Caponata Lasagna

Jewish Style Noodle Pudding with Prunes

Vegetable-Barley Moussaka

Middle Eastern Casserole

Moroccan Stew

Szechuan Vegetable-Tofu Stir-Fry

Vegetables Paprikash

COLOMBIAN STYLE VEGETABLE PLATE WITH SPICY TOMATO SAUCE

This type of sauce is often served over green beans and potatoes in Colombia. We made it into a vegetable plate by adding two more typical vegetables. If desired, add another—sweet potatoes, for example. Take care to cook each vegetable very soft when making a vegetable plate.

Serves 4

1½ pounds small red potatoes, unpeeled
1 pound green beans, ends trimmed
2 cups peeled, cubed (1 inch) butternut squash
4 ears corn, cut in 2-inch lengths (use frozen if fresh is not available)
2 cups peeled, sliced (1/3 inch) sweet potatoes (optional)

Spicy Tomato Sauce

2 tablespoons reduced-calorie margarine
2 scallions, green and white parts, minced
2/3 cup minced onion
1 can (1 pound) peeled tomatoes with liquid
1/4 teaspoon salt
1/4 teaspoon dried oregano
1/4 teaspoon pepper
1/8 teaspoon dried cumin
1/2 cup plus 2 tablespoons minced cilantro leaves (divided)
2/3 cup evaporated skim milk

1. Cook vegetables in 2 inches simmering water until very tender. Red potatoes should take 9 minutes, green beans 9 minutes, squash about 10 minutes, and corn sections about 5 minutes. (Optional sweet potatoes take about 10 minutes.) Drain well and place in attractive mounds in 9 x 13-inch ovenproof casserole. Heat oven to 350 degrees.

2. Make spicy tomato sauce: Melt margarine in large nonstick skillet over medium heat. Add scallions and onion and saute 4–5 minutes. Add tomatoes with liquid, squeezing each tomato with hands to break it into little pieces.

3. Add salt, oregano, pepper, cumin, and 2 tablespoons cilantro. Simmer 8–9 minutes until some of the liquid evaporates. Stir in milk and heat, stirring, for 1 minute more. Sauce should be thick.

4. Spoon sauce over vegetables, cover casserole, and place in oven. Bake at 350 degrees for 20 minutes or until vegetables and sauce are steaming hot. Uncover casserole and sprinkle remaining $1/2$ cup cilantro over vegetables. Bring to table; divide among 4 dinner plates and serve immediately.

Nutritional Data

PER SERVING		EXCHANGES	
Calories:	511	Milk:	0.5
% Calories from fat:	10	Vegetable:	3.0
Fat (gm):	5.9	Fruit:	0.0
Sat. fat (gm):	0.7	Bread:	5.0
Cholesterol (mg):	1.3	Meat:	0.0
Sodium (mg):	471	Fat:	1.0
Protein (gm):	16		
Carbohydrate (gm):	107.8		

NORMANDY VEGETABLES WITH NORMANDY SAUCE

We've substituted rutabaga for the hard-to-find salsify in this classic Normandy dish. And we suggest serving it with heated French bread and cold cider.

Serves 4

2½ cups cauliflower florets
2 cups peeled, diced (½ inch) rutabaga
2 cups peeled, cut up baby carrots
4 baking potatoes (8 ounces each), peeled, cut in ⅓-inch slices
2 cups peeled, diced (½ inch) celery root (celeriac)
Salt, to taste
White pepper, to taste
Normandy Sauce (recipe follows)

1. Cook vegetables in 2 inches simmering water until very tender. Cauliflower, rutabaga, and potatoes should take 7–8 minutes, carrots 9–10 minutes, celery root 8–10 minutes. Test with fork for tenderness and increase cooking time as needed.

2. Drain and divide vegetables evenly among 4 dinner plates, arranging them attractively. Lightly salt and pepper vegetables. Spoon Normandy Sauce over each serving.

Normandy Sauce

2 tablespoons reduced-calorie margarine
¼ cup finely minced onion
2 tablespoons plus 1 teaspoon flour
⅔ cup apple cider
⅔ cup dry white wine
¼ teaspoon salt
⅛ teaspoon white pepper
⅛ teaspoon ground nutmeg
⅔ cup evaporated skim milk
⅛ teaspoon fresh lemon juice
6 tablespoons chopped parsley leaves

1. Heat margarine in saucepan over medium heat. Saute onion 3 minutes. Add flour and cook, stirring, about 1 minute or until mixture turns a golden color. Mixture will be dry.

2. Add cider and wine, stirring constantly. Add salt, pepper, and nutmeg. Simmer 4–5 minutes or until thick. Add milk and lower heat slightly. Do not let mixture boil. Stir in lemon juice.

3. Spoon 1/2 cup sauce over each plate of vegetables, and sprinkle with 1 1/2 tablespoons parsley.

Nutritional Data

PER SERVING		EXCHANGES	
Calories:	423	Milk:	0.5
% Calories from fat:	8	Vegetable:	3.0
Fat (gm):	3.8	Fruit:	0.5
Sat. fat (gm):	0.7	Bread:	3.5
Cholesterol (mg):	1.3	Meat:	0.0
Sodium (mg):	371	Fat:	0.5
Protein (gm):	11.8		
Carbohydrate (gm):	83.2		

IRISH COLCANNON

This delicious Irish specialty is traditionally eaten on Halloween night. Although it's correctly made with kale, cabbage is often substituted. The potatoes are usually boiled; but we think the final mash is fluffier if they're baked instead. Serve it as an entree with Baked Tomatoes (see pg. 168) on the side.

Serves 4

2 pounds baking potatoes
4 cups chopped cabbage
6 green onions, green and white parts, minced
1/4 cup reduced-calorie margarine (divided)
1/2 cup evaporated skim milk
1/2 teaspoon salt
1/4 teaspoon pepper
　Pinch dried mace
2 tablespoons minced parsley leaves

1. Preheat oven to 350 degrees. Bake potatoes 1 hour or until insides are tender and fluffy. Meanwhile, fill a large saucepan with water, heat to boil, and add cabbage. Simmer 8 minutes. Drain in colander.

2. Scoop insides of potatoes out of jackets and place in electric mixing bowl. Discard jackets. Beat potatoes with 2 tablespoons margarine. Beat in milk, salt, pepper, and mace.

3. Melt remaining 2 tablespoons margarine over medium heat in large nonstick skillet. Add drained cabbage/scallion mixture and saute 3–4 minutes. Spoon into potato mixture and beat until well combined. Spoon colcannon into serving bowl and sprinkle with parsley. Bring to table with Baked Tomatoes (see pg. 168) if desired.

Nutritional Data

PER SERVING		EXCHANGES	
Calories:	319	Milk:	0.0
% Calories from fat:	17	Vegetable:	1.0
Fat (gm):	6.2	Fruit:	0.0
Sat. fat (gm):	1.1	Bread:	3.5
Cholesterol (mg):	1	Meat:	0.0
Sodium (mg):	463	Fat:	1.0
Protein (gm):	8.3		
Carbohydrate (gm):	59.9		

ITALIAN CAPONATA ON CABBAGE

We've taken a famous Italian classic—sweet-and-sour caponata—and used it as a sauce for braised cabbage.

Serves 6

1¼ cups water
1¼ cups white wine
1 vegetable bouillon cube
1 cabbage (3 pounds), cored, cut in ⅛-inch slices
Caponata Sauce (recipe follows)

1. Preheat oven to 325 degrees. Combine water, wine, and bouillon. Add cabbage and heat to boiling. Reduce heat to simmer, cover, and cook 30 minutes. Uncover and simmer another 30 minutes or until liquid has evaporated and cabbage is tender.

2. Divide cooked cabbage (about 4 cups) among 6 serving plates, spooning about ⅔ cup onto each plate. Spoon 1 cup (scant) hot caponata sauce over each helping of cabbage. Serve immediately.

Caponata Sauce

2 tablespoons reduced-calorie margarine
1 cup finely chopped red onion
1 red bell pepper, finely chopped
1 green bell pepper, finely chopped
1 cup peeled, finely chopped celery
4 cups finely chopped eggplant, baby if possible
1 can (1 pound) peeled tomatoes, coarsely chopped, with liquid
½ cup raisins
⅓ cup finely chopped green olives
5 tablespoons red wine vinegar
3 tablespoons sugar
2 tablespoons capers, drained
½ teaspoon salt (optional)
¼ teaspoon pepper
⅓ cup water

1. Heat margarine over medium heat in large nonstick skillet. Add onion, peppers, and celery and saute 5 minutes, stirring often. Add eggplant and saute 5 minutes more.

2. Add tomatoes with liquid. Add raisins, olives, vinegar, sugar, capers, (optional) salt, pepper, and ⅓ cup water. Simmer 20 minutes. Serve hot.

Nutritional Data

PER SERVING		EXCHANGES	
Calories:	219	Milk:	0.0
% Calories from fat:	15	Vegetable:	4.0
Fat (gm):	4	Fruit:	0.5
Sat. fat (gm):	0.6	Bread:	1.0
Cholesterol (mg):	0	Meat:	0.0
Sodium (mg):	688	Fat:	0.5
Protein (gm):	4.7		
Carbohydrate (gm):	38.8		

CAPONATA LASAGNA

This dish uses the famous Italian sweet-and-sour caponata sauce as a lasagna filling. Serve with heated Italian bread, if desired.

Serves 8

Caponata Sauce (see preceding recipe), withhold salt
3 cups fat-free ricotta cheese (divided)
½ cup evaporated skim milk
12 lasagna noodles (10 ounces) cooked, drained, (divided)
2 cups (8 ounces) shredded reduced-fat mozzarella cheese (divided)
6 tablespoons grated Parmesan cheese (divided)

1. Make Caponata Sauce: See preceding recipe. Withhold salt.

2. Assemble casserole. Preheat oven to 350 degrees. Mix ricotta and milk. Spoon ¼ of caponata sauce (about 1⅓ cups) over bottom of 13 x 9-inch casserole or ovenproof dish. Top with 4 lasagna noodles, overlapping slightly. Use spatula to spread 1 cup ricotta on noodles in thin layer. Sprinkle ⅔ cup mozzarella over ricotta. Sprinkle 2 tablespoons Parmesan over mozzarella. Repeat second layer with caponata sauce, lasagna, ricotta, mozzarella, and Parmesan.

3. Arrange final layer as follows: 1$\frac{1}{3}$ cups caponata sauce, 4 noodles, 1 cup ricotta, remaining caponata sauce, $\frac{2}{3}$ cup mozzarella, and 2 tablespoons Parmesan.

4. Cover casserole loosely with foil. Bake 30 minutes or until bubbly. Remove foil and bake 15 minutes longer. Let rest 15 minutes at room temperature before serving.

Nutritional Data

PER SERVING		EXCHANGES	
Calories:	333	Milk:	0.0
% Calories from fat:	21	Vegetable:	2.0
Fat (gm):	8.2	Fruit:	0.5
Sat. fat (gm):	1.3	Bread:	1.5
Cholesterol (mg):	23.3	Meat:	2.5
Sodium (mg):	674	Fat:	0.0
Protein (gm):	27.6		
Carbohydrate (gm):	43.6		

JEWISH STYLE NOODLE PUDDING WITH PRUNES

Serves 8

Vegetable cooking spray
$\frac{1}{2}$ pound pitted prunes, halved with scissors
1$\frac{1}{2}$ cups water
1 tablespoon lemon juice
2 tablespoons sugar
6 cups cooked egg noodles, drained
$\frac{1}{8}$ teaspoon white pepper
$\frac{1}{2}$ teaspoon salt (optional)
4 cups 1% cottage cheese, no-salt-added type
2 large eggs, beaten
$\frac{1}{2}$ cup egg substitute, or 2 eggs
$\frac{1}{2}$ cup evaporated skim milk
$\frac{3}{4}$ teaspoon salt (optional)
$\frac{1}{4}$ cup sugar (optional)
$\frac{1}{4}$ cup reduced-calorie margarine

1⅓ cups breadcrumbs, made in food processor or
blender from reduced-calorie white bread

1. Preheat oven to 350 degrees. Spray 9 x 13-inch glass casserole with
   nonstick cooking spray.

2. Place prunes in heavy-bottomed saucepan with water, lemon juice, and
   2 tablespoons sugar. Heat to boiling, then simmer 15 minutes or until
   prunes are very soft. Strain prunes, pressing gently with wooden
   spoon to extract excess liquid.

3. Place noodles in bowl and toss with white pepper and (optional)
   ½ teaspoon salt.

4. Combine cottage cheese with eggs, egg substitute, and milk. Add
   (optional) ¾ teaspoon salt. Add (optional) ¼ cup sugar.

5. Spoon 2 cups noodles on bottom of prepared casserole. Arrange half of
   prunes over noodles, remembering to fill edges and corners. Spoon
   half of cheese mixture over prunes. Spoon another 2 cups noodles
   over cheese; top with remaining prunes; spoon remaining cheese over
   prunes. Spoon remaining noodles over cheese.

6. Melt margarine and combine with breadcrumbs. Strew crumbs over
   casserole, covering as evenly as possible. Bake 35 minutes until
   crumbs are golden. Cut in half lengthwise. Cut each half into 4 pieces.

Nutritional Data

PER SERVING		EXCHANGES	
Calories:	413	Milk:	0.0
% Calories from fat:	16	Vegetable:	0.0
Fat (gm):	7.3	Fruit:	1.5
Sat. fat (gm):	1.3	Bread:	2.5
Cholesterol (mg):	93.5	Meat:	2.5
Sodium (mg):	208	Fat:	0.0
Protein (gm):	25.1		
Carbohydrate (gm):	60.8		

VEGETABLE-BARLEY MOUSSAKA

This meatless version of traditional moussaka is filled with sumptuous vegetables and hearty barley, topped with a creamy custard.

Serves 12

1 large eggplant, unpeeled, sliced
Olive oil cooking spray
1 pound potatoes, unpeeled, sliced
3 cups chopped onions
8 ounces carrots, sliced
3 cloves garlic, minced
1 teaspoon dried cinnamon
1 teaspoon dried oregano
1/2 teaspoon dried thyme
3/4 cup vegetable broth
2 cups chopped tomatoes
2 cups sliced mushrooms
2 cups cooked barley
1 small zucchini, sliced
Salt, to taste
Pepper, to taste
Custard Topping (recipe follows)
Ground nutmeg, to taste

1. Spray eggplant slices on both sides with cooking spray. Bake in sprayed aluminum-foil-lined jellyroll pan at 350 degrees until tender but still firm to touch, about 20 minutes. Arrange eggplant on bottom of 13 x 9 x 2-inch baking pan.

2. Heat potatoes, onions, carrots, garlic, cinnamon, oregano, thyme, and vegetable broth to boiling in large skillet; reduce heat and simmer, uncovered, 3–5 minutes. Add tomatoes and mushrooms; simmer, uncovered, until tomatoes are soft. Add barley and zucchini; cook, uncovered, until mixture is thick. Season to taste with salt and pepper.

3. Spoon vegetable mixture over eggplant. Pour Custard Topping over and sprinkle with nutmeg. Bake at 350 degrees until lightly browned on the top, about 45 minutes. Cool 5–10 minutes before cutting.

Custard Topping

⅓ cup margarine
½ cup all purpose flour
3 cups skim milk
1 egg
2 egg whites
½ teaspoon salt (optional)
⅛ teaspoon white pepper

1. Melt margarine in medium saucepan; stir in flour. Cook over medium heat until bubbly, about 2 minutes, stirring constantly. Stir in milk; heat to boiling. Boil stirring constantly until thickened, about 1 minute.

2. Beat egg and egg whites in small bowl. Stir about 1 cup milk mixture into eggs; stir egg mixture back into saucepan. Stir in pepper and (optional) salt. Cook over low heat until thickened, 2–3 minutes.

Nutritional Data

PER SERVING		EXCHANGES	
Calories:	207	Milk:	0.0
% Calories from fat:	26	Vegetable:	2.0
Fat (gm):	6.2	Fruit:	0.0
Sat. fat (gm):	1.3	Bread:	1.5
Cholesterol (mg):	18.8	Meat:	0.0
Sodium (mg):	141	Fat:	1.0
Protein (gm):	7		
Carbohydrate (gm):	32.6		

MIDDLE EASTERN CASSEROLE

Serves 4

$1/2$ pound large carrots, peeled, cut lengthwise into slices, each $1/4$ inch thick

1 cup peeled, seeded, coarsely chopped tomatoes

$2/3$ cup chopped red onion

6 tablespoons minced green bell pepper

6 tablespoons minced red bell pepper

$1/3$ cup minced parsley

$1/3$ cup minced cilantro

4 teaspoons minced fresh dill (divided)

1 teaspoon finely minced garlic

1 teaspoon sugar

$1/2$ teaspoon salt plus enough for light sprinkling* of each layer

$1/2$ teaspoon pepper plus enough for light sprinkling* of each layer

$1/2$ pound baby eggplant, cut lengthwise into slices, each $1/4$ inch thick

$1/2$ pound zucchini, cut lengthwise into slices, each $1/4$ inch thick

$1/2$ pound potatoes, peeled, cut lengthwise into slices, each $1/4$ inch thick

1. Preheat oven to 350 degrees. Place carrots in dish with 2 tablespoons water, and microwave on high 5 minutes. Drain.

2. Place tomatoes, red onion, red and green bell peppers, parsley, cilantro, 2 teaspoons dill, garlic, sugar, salt, and pepper in bowl and stir well to combine.

3. Cover bottom of shallow, flat-bottomed, 6-cup ovenproof casserole with carrot slices. Sprinkle lightly with salt and pepper. Top with a scant $2/3$ cup of vegetable mixture over carrots. Cover with eggplant slices and add another light sprinkling of salt and pepper. Top with another scant $2/3$ cup vegetable mixture over eggplant.

4. Place zucchini slices over vegetable mixture, add another light sprinkle of salt and pepper, and top with scant $2/3$ cup vegetable mixture.

Finish with potatoes, sprinkling of salt and pepper, and remaining vegetable mixture.

5. Cover casserole or top securely with foil. Bake 1 hour or until vegetables are fork-tender. Remove from oven and let rest 10 minutes at room temperature. Sprinkle top with remaining 2 teaspoons dill before bringing to table.

*Note: Sprinklings of salt and pepper are not included in nutritional data.

Nutritional Data

PER SERVING		EXCHANGES	
Calories:	144	Milk:	0.0
% Calories from fat:	4	Vegetable:	3.0
Fat (gm):	0.7	Fruit:	0.0
Sat. fat (gm):	0.1	Bread:	1.0
Cholesterol (mg):	0	Meat:	0.0
Sodium (mg):	320	Fat:	0.0
Protein (gm):	4		
Carbohydrate (gm):	36.3		

MOROCCAN STEW

Enjoy the subtle blending of curry, cumin, and cinnamon in this fragrant vegetable stew from northern Africa.

Serves 6

1½ cups chopped onion
2 cloves garlic, minced
1 tablespoon olive oil, *or* vegetable oil
¾ teaspoon dried cinnamon
½ teaspoon curry powder
½ teaspoon dried cumin
¼ teaspoon ground nutmeg
¼ teaspoon cayenne
10 ounces fresh or frozen (thawed) whole okra
2 cups peeled, cubed sweet potatoes
1 medium zucchini, cubed
1 medium red bell pepper, coarsely chopped
1 cup cubed unpeeled eggplant
½ cup vegetable broth
1 cup fresh or frozen (thawed) peas

1 can (15½ ounces) garbanzo beans, rinsed, drained
2 medium tomatoes, chopped
⅓ cup dark raisins
Salt, to taste
Pepper, to taste
Cilantro Rice (recipe follows)
Cilantro, *or* parsley, leaves, finely chopped

1. Saute onions and garlic in oil in large saucepan until tender, about 5 minutes. Stir in spices; cook 2–3 minutes. Stir in okra, sweet potatoes, zucchini, bell pepper, eggplant, and broth; heat to boiling. Reduce heat and simmer, covered, 5 minutes.

2. Add peas, beans, tomatoes, and raisins; simmer, covered, until vegetables are tender, about 20 minutes. Season to taste with salt and pepper. Serve stew over Cilantro Rice; sprinkle with cilantro.

Cilantro Rice

Makes about 8 cups

4½ cups water
1 teaspoon dried turmeric
½ teaspoon salt
2 cups converted white rice, uncooked
¼ cup finely chopped cilantro, *or* parsley, leaves

1. Heat water, turmeric, and salt to boiling in large saucepan; stir in rice. Reduce heat and simmer, covered, until rice is tender, about 25 minutes. Stir in cilantro.

Nutritional Data

PER SERVING		EXCHANGES	
Calories:	348	Milk:	0.0
% Calories from fat:	12	Vegetable:	2.0
Fat (gm):	4.6	Fruit:	0.5
Sat. fat (gm):	0.7	Bread:	3.5
Cholesterol (mg):	0	Meat:	0.0
Sodium (mg):	523	Fat:	0.5
Protein (gm):	10.2		
Carbohydrate (gm):	69.5		

SZECHUAN VEGETABLE-TOFU STIR-FRY

Hot chili oil is available in the oriental sections of supermarkets. The flavor is hot, so adjust the amount according to your taste preference.

Serves 4

1 cup vegetable broth (divided)
2–3 dried Chinese black mushrooms
1/4 cup orange juice
1/4 cup reduced-sodium soy sauce
2 teaspoons hot chili oil (divided)
1/2 teaspoon pepper
4 ounces firm tofu, drained, cubed (3/4 inch)
1 tablespoon cornstarch
1 tablespoon vegetable oil
2 teaspoons grated ginger root
2 cloves garlic, minced
1 cup chopped bok choy (Chinese cabbage)
2 medium carrots, diagonally sliced
1/2 cup sliced green onion, green and white parts
1/2 medium red bell pepper, coarsely chopped
1/2 cup cauliflower florets
1/2 cup broccoli florets
1 ounce snow peas, ends trimmed
6 cups cooked rice, warm
1 teaspoon toasted sesame seeds

1. Heat 1/2 cup broth to boiling; pour over mushrooms in small bowl. Let stand until mushrooms are soft, about 10 minutes. Drain mushrooms, reserving broth. Slice mushrooms, discarding tough stems, and reserve.

2. Combine remaining 1/2 cup broth, orange juice, soy sauce, 1 teaspoon chili oil, and pepper; pour over tofu in bowl. Let stand 15–60 minutes stirring occasionally. Remove tofu and reserve. Stir cornstarch into soy broth and reserve.

3. Heat remaining 1 teaspoon hot chili oil and vegetable oil in wok or large skillet until hot. Add ginger root and garlic and stir-fry 1 minute.

Add bok choy, carrots, green onions, bell pepper, cauliflower, broccoli, and reserved mushrooms; stir-fry 5–7 minutes. Add snow peas and reserved broth; cook, covered, 2–3 minutes until vegetables are crisp-tender.

4. Add reserved soy broth mixture to wok and heat to boiling, stirring constantly, until thickened. Add tofu; cook until hot, 1–2 minutes. Spoon mixture over rice; sprinkle with sesame seeds.

Nutritional Data

PER SERVING		EXCHANGES	
Calories:	483	Milk:	0.0
% Calories from fat:	18	Vegetable:	2.0
Fat (gm):	9.5	Fruit:	0.0
Sat. fat (gm):	1.3	Bread:	5.0
Cholesterol (mg):	0	Meat:	0.0
Sodium (mg):	579	Fat:	1.5
Protein (gm):	15.2		
Carbohydrate (gm):	84.1		

VEGETABLES PAPRIKASH

Your preference of hot or sweet paprika can be used in this recipe. Serve over any pasta (flat shape preferred) or rice.

Serves 4

2 cups thinly sliced cabbage
2 medium onions, sliced
1 medium zucchini, sliced
2 medium carrots, sliced
2 medium green bell peppers, sliced
1 tablespoon olive oil, *or* vegetable oil
1½ cups sliced mushrooms
1 medium tomato, chopped
3 tablespoons flour
1 tablespoon paprika
¾ cup vegetable broth
½ cup fat-free sour cream
Salt, to taste
Pepper, to taste
12 ounces no-yolk noodles, cooked, warm

1. Saute cabbage, onions, zucchini, carrots, and green peppers in oil in large skillet until tender, 5 to 8 minutes. Add mushrooms and tomatoes. Cook over medium heat, covered, until cabbage and tomatoes are wilted.

2. Stir in flour and paprika; cook 1–2 minutes, stirring constantly. Stir in broth; cook until sauce thickens. Stir in sour cream; season to taste with salt and pepper. Serve over noodles.

Nutritional Data

PER SERVING		EXCHANGES	
Calories:	261	Milk:	0.0
% Calories from fat:	16	Vegetable:	3.0
Fat (gm):	5	Fruit:	0.0
Sat. fat (gm):	0.7	Bread:	2.0
Cholesterol (mg):	0	Meat:	0.0
Sodium (mg):	126	Fat:	1.0
Protein (gm):	9.7		
Carbohydrate (gm):	48.2		

12
DISHES FOR ENTERTAINING

Lentil Ravioli with Gingered Tomato Relish

Root Vegetable Platter with Rémoulade

Baked Tomatoes

Stuffed Portobello Mushrooms

Squash and Mushroom Galette

Spaghetti Squash with Wine, Orange, and Squash Sauce

Vegetable Plate with Tofu Aioli

3-Foot Submarine with Roasted Vegetables

Cabbage-Fennel Strudel

LENTIL RAVIOLI WITH GINGERED TOMATO RELISH

Delicate ravioli, bursting with myriad flavors! For luncheon portions, this recipe will serve 6 to 8 people.

Serves 4 (6 ravioli each)

Olive oil cooking spray
1/4 cup finely chopped fennel bulb, *or* celery
2 teaspoons grated ginger root
1 teaspoon curry powder
1/2 teaspoon dried cumin
1/4 teaspoon dried turmeric
1/4 teaspoon dried cinnamon
1/4 teaspoon cayenne
2 2/3 cups water
2/3 cup dried lentils, cleaned, rinsed
2 tablespoons finely chopped cilantro leaves
Salt, to taste
48 wonton wrappers
Gingered Tomato Relish (recipe follows)
Cilantro, *or* parsley, sprigs for garnish

1. Spray large skillet and heat over medium heat until hot. Saute fennel and ginger root 2–3 minutes; add spices and cook 1 minute longer.

2. Add water and lentils to skillet; heat to boiling. Reduce heat and simmer, covered, until lentils are just tender, about 15 minutes. Simmer uncovered, until excess liquid is gone, about 5 minutes. Stir in chopped cilantro; season to taste with salt.

3. Place 1 tablespoon lentil mixture in center of 1 wonton wrapper; brush edges of wrapper with water. Place second wonton wrapper on top and press edges to seal. Repeat with remaining wonton wrappers and filling.

4. Heat about 3 quarts water to boiling in large saucepan; add 4 to 6 ravioli. Reduce heat and simmer, uncovered, until ravioli float to surface and are cooked *al dente,* 3 to 4 minutes. Remove ravioli with slotted spoon; repeat cooking procedure with remaining ravioli.

5. Arrange ravioli on plates and top with Gingered Tomato Relish; garnish with cilantro.

Gingered Tomato Relish

Makes about 1¹/₂ cups

1¹/₂ cups chopped tomatoes
¹/₂ cup finely chopped zucchini
¹/₄ cup finely chopped carrot
¹/₄ cup finely chopped onion
1 tablespoon grated ginger root
Salt, to taste
Pepper, to taste

1. Combine all ingredients, except salt and pepper, in medium skillet. Cook, covered, over medium heat until tomatoes are soft and mixture is bubbly. Simmer, uncovered, until excess liquid is gone, about 10 minutes. Season to taste with salt and pepper

Nutritional Data

PER SERVING		EXCHANGES	
Calories:	354	Milk:	0.0
% Calories from fat:	5	Vegetable:	2.0
Fat (gm):	1.9	Fruit:	0.0
Sat. fat (gm):	0.3	Bread:	4.0
Cholesterol (mg):	12	Meat:	0.0
Sodium (mg):	568	Fat:	0.0
Protein (gm):	14.4		
Carbohydrate (gm):	70.1		

ROOT VEGETABLE PLATTER WITH RÉMOULADE

This recipe, intended for 8 people, can easily grow or shrink to accommodate any number of guests. Choose any four (or more) vegetables from the list—but be sure to include white potatoes in any platter. If desired, add bread and reduced-calorie cheese.

Serves 8

4 cups peeled, sliced beets
4 cups peeled, sliced turnips,* *or* rutabagas,
     or parsnips
4 cups cubed carrots,* *or* kohlrabi
4 cups peeled, cubed celery root
4 cups peeled, sliced Idaho potatoes*
4 cups peeled, sliced sweet potatoes*
8 hard-cooked eggs, halved lengthwise (optional)
   Salt, to taste
   Pepper, to taste
½ cup minced parsley leaves, as garnish
   Tofu Rémoulade (recipe follows)

1. Select 4 vegetables; cut them as indicated or any way you wish, including several different shapes such as cubes, slices, half-slices, etc., to make the platter more interesting. Steam vegetables, or cook in 2 inches simmering water until tender; drain.

2. Arrange vegetables attractively on serving platter; garnish with (optional) egg halves. Season vegetables to taste with salt and pepper and sprinkle with parsley. Serve with Tofu Rémoulade.

Tofu Rémoulade

Makes about 2½ cups

2 cups soft tofu
¼ cup canola oil
4 teaspoons lemon juice
½ teaspoon salt
½ teaspoon dried turmeric
½ teaspoon dry mustard
¼ teaspoon white pepper

¼ teaspoon cayenne
¼ cup minced parsley leaves
2 tablespoons sweet pickle relish
4 teaspoons minced green onion tops
4 teaspoons drained capers

1. Process tofu, oil, lemon juice, salt, turmeric, dry mustard, white pepper, and cayenne in food processor or blender until smooth. Stir in parsley, relish, green onion tops, and capers.

*Note: Vegetables with an asterisk (*) were used to compile the nutritional data. Vegetables can be cooked in advance; rinse under cold water to stop cooking. Arrange on heatproof platter and refrigerate, covered with aluminum foil. To reheat, place in 350-degree oven until hot, about 20 minutes. Tofu Rémoulade can be refrigerated up to 1 week; serve at room temperature.

Nutritional Data

PER SERVING		EXCHANGES	
Calories:	359	Milk:	0.0
% Calories from fat:	22	Vegetable:	3.0
Fat (gm):	9.2	Fruit:	0.0
Sat. fat (gm):	0.8	Bread:	3.0
Cholesterol (mg):	0	Meat:	0.0
Sodium (mg):	301	Fat:	1.5
Protein (gm):	8.7		
Carbohydrate (gm):	63.8		

BAKED TOMATOES

This side dish is especially good with Onion Quiche on pg. 114,
but it can be served with any entree of your choice.

Serves 8

4 teaspoons reduced-calorie margarine (divided)
3 tablespoons finely minced red onions
⅛ teaspoon salt
⅛ teaspoon dried thyme
　Pinch dried basil
　Pinch pepper
3 slices reduced-calorie white bread
1 tablespoon grated Parmesan cheese
4 firm tomatoes, cored, halved
　Salt and pepper, to taste

1. Preheat oven to 350 degrees. Melt 2 teaspoons margarine in small saucepan over medium heat. Saute onions 4–5 minutes.

2. Add ⅛ teaspoon salt, thyme, pinch of basil, and pinch of pepper, mixing well. Remove from heat. Make bread into crumbs in food processor or blender. Melt remaining 2 teaspoons margarine and stir it, breadcrumbs, and Parmesan cheese into onion mixture.

3. Arrange tomatoes, cut sides up, in shallow, ovenproof baking dish. Sprinkle lightly with salt and pepper to taste. Spoon about 2½ tablespoons onion/crumb mixture onto each tomato.

4. Bake tomatoes 25 minutes or until crumbs are golden brown. Serve warm or at room temperature. Use spatula to lift tomatoes.

Nutritional Data

PER SERVING		EXCHANGES	
Calories:	44	Milk:	0.0
% Calories from fat:	30	Vegetable:	0.5
Fat (gm):	1.6	Fruit:	0.0
Sat. fat (gm):	0.4	Bread:	0.5
Cholesterol (mg):	0.6	Meat:	0.0
Sodium (mg):	114	Fat:	0.0
Protein (gm):	1.6		
Carbohydrate (gm):	7		

STUFFED PORTOBELLO MUSHROOMS

These entree-size mushrooms can also be served as appetizers: select a smaller size, or cut large mushrooms into halves or quarters.

Serves 4 (2 mushrooms each)

    8 large portobello mushrooms (5 or more inches
      in diameter)
      Vegetable cooking spray
    1 cup chopped red bell pepper
    1 cup chopped yellow bell pepper
  1/2 cup chopped shallot, *or* onion
  1/4 cup thinly sliced green onions and tops
    6 cloves garlic, minced
  1/2 teaspoon dried basil
  1/2 teaspoon dried marjoram
1/4–1/2 teaspoon dried thyme
      Salt and pepper, to taste
    6 ounces shredded fat-free mozzarella, *or*
      Cheddar, cheese
    2 ounces goat's cheese, crumbled
      Finely chopped basil, *or* parsley, leaves as
      garnish

1. Remove mushroom stems, chop, and reserve. Bake mushrooms, smooth sides down, in greased large jellyroll pan at 425 degrees for 15 minutes.

2. Spray large skillet with cooking spray; heat over medium heat until hot. Saute mushroom stems, bell pepper, shallot, green onions, and garlic until tender, 8–10 minutes. Stir in herbs and cook 1–2 minutes longer; season to taste with salt and pepper.

3. Spoon vegetable mixture into mushrooms; sprinkle with cheeses. Bake at 425 degrees until mushrooms are tender and cheeses melted, about 10 minutes. Garnish with basil or parsley.

Nutritional Data

PER SERVING		EXCHANGES	
Calories:	189	Milk:	0.0
% Calories from fat:	25	Vegetable:	1.5
Fat (gm):	5.6	Fruit:	0.0
Sat. fat (gm):	3.5	Bread:	0.5
Cholesterol (mg):	15	Meat:	2.0
Sodium (mg):	353	Fat:	0.0
Protein (gm):	21.9		
Carbohydrate (gm):	14.8		

SQUASH AND MUSHROOM GALETTE

*Any flavorful wild mushroom, such as shiitake, oyster,
or cremini, can be substituted for the portobello mushrooms.
This elegant entree tart can also be cut into smaller
wedges and served as a first course.*

Serves 4

- 1 pound acorn, *or* butternut, squash, cut in halves, seeds discarded
- 1/2 cup thinly sliced leek, white parts only
- 1 small onion, chopped
- 1 medium red bell pepper, chopped
- 2 portobello mushrooms, sliced
- 8 cloves garlic, minced
- 1 1/2 teaspoons dried sage
- 1 tablespoon olive oil, *or* vegetable oil
  Salt, to taste
  Pepper, to taste
  Pastry Dough (recipe follows)
- 1/2 cup shredded fat-free Cheddar cheese
- 2 tablespoons grated Parmesan cheese
- 1 egg white, beaten

1. Place squash, cut sides down, in baking pan. Bake at 375 degrees until very tender, about 1 hour. Scoop squash from shells and mash with fork, in large bowl.

2. Saute leek, onion, bell pepper, mushrooms, garlic, and sage in oil in large skillet until tender, about 5 minutes. Mix into squash; season to taste with salt and pepper.

3. Roll Pastry Dough on lightly floured surface to 14-inch circle; transfer to cookie sheet or large pizza pan. Spoon vegetable mixture evenly on dough, leaving 2-inch border around side. Sprinkle with cheeses. Fold edge of dough over edge of vegetable mixture, pleating to fit.

4. Brush edge of dough with beaten egg white. Bake at 400 degrees until dough is golden, about 25 minutes. Cut into wedges; serve warm.

Pastry Dough

    1 teaspoon active dry yeast
  1/3 cup warm water (115 degrees)
    1 egg, beaten
    3 tablespoons fat-free sour cream
 1 1/2 cups all-purpose flour
  1/4 teaspoon salt

1. Stir yeast into warm water in medium bowl; let stand 5 minutes. Add egg and sour cream to yeast mixture, mixing until smooth. Stir in flour and salt, making a soft dough. Knead dough on lightly floured surface until smooth, 1–2 minutes.

Nutritional Data

PER SERVING		EXCHANGES	
Calories:	339	Milk:	0.0
% Calories from fat:	18	Vegetable:	1.0
Fat (gm):	7.1	Fruit:	0.0
Sat. fat (gm):	1.7	Bread:	3.0
Cholesterol (mg):	58.3	Meat:	1.0
Sodium (mg):	338	Fat:	1.0
Protein (gm):	16.5		
Carbohydrate (gm):	54		

SPAGHETTI SQUASH WITH WINE, ORANGE, AND SQUASH SAUCE

Spaghetti squash resembles spaghetti after it's cooked because it separates into individual strands. But because it has such a delicate flavor, we decided to forgo the traditional spaghetti tomato sauce and include instead a delicate wine and orange sauce.

Serves 6

- 3 cups peeled, coarsely chopped butternut squash
- 3 tablespoons reduced-calorie margarine
- 3 tablespoons minced shallot, *or* onions
- 2/3 teaspoon salt
- 3 cups dry white wine
- 3 cups orange juice
- 3 spaghetti squash (about 2 pounds each), split lengthwise
- 6 tablespoons chopped cilantro, *or* parsley, leaves

1. Steam butternut squash, or cook in 2 inches simmering water until very soft. Drain and reserve squash in food processor or blender container.

2. Meanwhile, melt margarine in large saucepan, add shallots, and saute 3 minutes. Add salt, wine, and orange juice. Simmer 20 minutes or until enough liquid evaporates so remainder measures 3 cups.

3. Pour wine and orange mixture into food processor or blender container, with butternut squash and puree until smooth. Return puree to saucepan. Preheat oven to 225 degrees.

4. Line bottom of microwave with paper towels. Cover each spaghetti squash half with plastic wrap. Place 3 halves, cut side up, in microwave. Microwave on high 9–10 minutes.

5. Remove plastic wrap and scoop out seeds. Scrape fork tines lightly over squash to see if "strands" fall into center cavity. If they do, squash is cooked. If not, cover again with plastic wrap and return to microwave for another minute or so.

6. Place cooked spaghetti squash on ovenproof platter, cut side down, and keep warm in oven while remaining squash halves are microwaved.

7. Arrange cooked spaghetti squash halves on serving platter, cut side up. Use fork tines to lightly scrape some squash strands into center cavities of squash halves. Spoon a generous half-cup of heated sauce into each squash, and sprinkle each with 1 tablespoon cilantro or parsley. Serve immediately.

Nutritional Data

PER SERVING		EXCHANGES	
Calories:	230	Milk:	0.0
% Calories from fat:	13	Vegetable:	1.0
Fat (gm):	3.6	Fruit:	2.0
Sat. fat (gm):	0.6	Bread:	0.5
Cholesterol (mg):	0	Meat:	0.0
Sodium (mg):	301	Fat:	0.5
Protein (gm):	3.2		
Carbohydrate (gm):	30.2		

VEGETABLE PLATE WITH TOFU AIOLI

The French word "aioli" refers to both garlic mayonnaise and to a French classic dish in which garlic mayonnaise is spooned over eggs and vegetables. Instead of basing our mayonnaise on eggs and oil, we use tofu. The result is very similar to mayonnaise and absolutely delicious. We defy you to tell the difference.

Serves 4

Tofu Aioli Sauce

1 cup soft tofu
2 tablespoons canola oil
1 teaspoon white wine vinegar
1 teaspoon lemon juice
1/4 teaspoon salt (optional)
1/4 teaspoon dried turmeric
1/4 teaspoon dry mustard
Large pinch white pepper
6 garlic cloves, peeled, coarsely chopped

1. Place tofu, oil, vinegar, lemon juice, (optional) salt, turmeric, mustard, and pepper in food processor. Pulse to combine. Add garlic and pulse until incorporated. Use immediately or store in refrigerator.

Vegetables

     2 packages (10 ounces each) frozen artichoke hearts
     1 pound green beans, ends trimmed
     2 cups peeled baby carrots
     4 red potatoes (about 5 ounces each), scrubbed, halved
     4 large eggs, hard cooked, halved lengthwise (optional)
       Salt, to taste
       Pepper, to taste
     6 tablespoons chopped parsley leaves

1. Cook artichoke hearts, green beans, carrots, and potatoes separately, each in 2 inches of simmering water. Artichokes should be tender in 7–8 minutes, beans in 8–9, carrots in 9–10, and potatoes in 15–20. Cook vegetables until tender, testing for tenderness with fork tines.

2. Arrange vegetables and (optional) eggs on 4 serving plates. Lightly salt and pepper vegetables to taste. Spoon aioli over vegetables, and sprinkle each serving with 1½ tablespoons parsley.

Nutritional Data

PER SERVING		EXCHANGES	
Calories:	463	Milk:	0.0
% Calories from fat:	24	Vegetable:	5.0
Fat (gm):	13	Fruit:	0.0
Sat. fat (gm):	1.8	Bread:	3.0
Cholesterol (mg):	0	Meat:	0.0
Sodium (mg):	457	Fat:	2.5
Protein (gm):	14.8		
Carbohydrate (gm):	79.8		

3-FOOT SUBMARINE WITH ROASTED VEGETABLES

This delicious sandwich is made with a 3-foot-long French bread and a tofu-based mayonnaise flavored with garlic and cayenne pepper.

Serves 12

Tofu Mayonnaise

2½ cups soft tofu
7½ tablespoons olive oil, *or* canola oil
2½ teaspoons white wine vinegar
2½ teaspoons fresh lemon juice
1¼ teaspoons salt (optional)
½ teaspoon plus ⅛ teaspoon dry mustard
½ teaspoon plus ⅛ teaspoon dried turmeric
1 teaspoon cayenne (add more if desired)
6 cloves garlic, coarsely chopped

1. Combine tofu, oil, vinegar, lemon juice, (optional) salt, dry mustard, turmeric, and cayenne in food processor container and pulse until well mixed. Add garlic and pulse until incorporated. Reserve at room temperature.

Sandwich

2 pounds eggplant, cut in ⅓-inch slices
8 medium bell peppers, all colors, cored, seeded, quartered
1 3-foot-long French bread*
1½ cups coarsely chopped cilantro leaves
8 leaves curly lettuce, green or red, washed, well dried
3 large, firm tomatoes, cut in ⅓-inch slices
Salt and pepper, to taste
4 ounces shredded reduced-fat sharp Cheddar cheese, *or* any reduced-fat cheese

1. Preheat oven to 400 degrees. Line 2 cookie sheets with baking parchment and place eggplant slices on parchment. Roast 15–20 minutes or until slices are very soft. Remove from oven and reserve.

2. Arrange bell pepper quarters on parchment and roast 15–20 minutes or until skins are loosened and peppers are soft. Allow to cool. Then remove skins and cut into slices.

3. Split bread lengthwise, using electric knife if possible. If desired, remove some bread from the "lid" half, but be sure to leave remaining shell at least 1 inch thick. Spread bottom and top halves of bread generously with Tofu Mayonnaise, using about 1 cup for each half. Reserve remaining ½ cup.

4. Sprinkle cilantro over bottom half of bread. Arrange lettuce in overlapping fashion on cilantro, curly edges out. Arrange tomato slices on lettuce. Lightly salt and pepper tomatoes to taste. Arrange eggplant slices on tomatoes.

5. Drizzle remaining ½ cup Tofu Mayonnaise over eggplant. Top with bell pepper slices. Lightly salt and pepper bell peppers to taste.

6. Sprinkle cheese over peppers. Add top half of bread to sandwich. Secure with sandwich picks if desired. Wrap sandwich completely in plastic wrap until ready to serve.

At serving time, cut sandwich into 2- or 3-inch sections, with electric knife if possible.

*Note: Three-foot breads (ours weighed 3 pounds and was 6¼ inches wide at the center) can be ordered at some supermarket or delicatessen counters, at local wholesale bakeries, or at shops that sell their own submarine and hero sandwiches. The sandwich should be served within an hour or two of making it or bread will become soggy from the mayonnaise.

Nutritional Data

PER SERVING		EXCHANGES	
Calories:	490	Milk:	0.0
% Calories from fat:	29	Vegetable:	2.0
Fat (gm):	15.8	Fruit:	0.0
Sat. fat (gm):	3.1	Bread:	4.0
Cholesterol (mg):	6.8	Meat:	1.0
Sodium (mg):	777	Fat:	2.0
Protein (gm):	17.3		
Carbohydrate (gm):	71.2		

CABBAGE-FENNEL STRUDEL

If fresh fennel is not available, substitute sliced celery and add ¹/₂ teaspoon crushed fennel seed to the recipe with the teaspoon of anise seed.

Serves 4

Vegetable cooking spray
1 cup chopped onions
¹/₂ cup sliced leek, *or* green onion, green and white parts
3 cloves garlic, minced
4 cups thinly sliced cabbage
1 cup sliced mushrooms
¹/₂ cup thinly sliced fennel bulb
1 cup vegetable broth
¹/₂ cup dry white wine, *or* vegetable broth
1 teaspoon crushed anise seed
¹/₂ teaspoon crushed caraway seed
³/₄ cup cooked brown rice
¹/₄ cup dark raisins
Salt, to taste
Pepper, to taste
6 sheets frozen filo pastry, thawed
Anise or caraway seed, to taste
Herb-Tomato Sauce (see pg. 32)

1. Spray large saucepan with cooking spray; heat over medium heat until hot. Add onion, leek, and garlic; saute 3–5 minutes. Add cabbage, mushrooms, fennel, broth, wine, and anise and caraway seeds; cook, covered, until cabbage wilts, 5 to 10 minutes. Cook, uncovered, over medium heat until cabbage begins to brown, about 10 minutes. Stir in rice and raisins; season to taste with salt and pepper. Cool.

2. Lay 1 sheet filo on clean surface; cover remaining filo with damp towel to keep from drying. Spray filo with cooking spray; top with 2 more sheets filo, spraying each with cooking spray Spoon ¹/₂ cabbage mixture across dough, 2 inches from short edge; roll up and place, seam-side down, on greased cookie sheet. Flatten roll slightly; spray with cooking spray and sprinkle with anise seed. Repeat with remaining filo and cabbage mixture.

3. Bake at 375 degrees until strudel is golden, 35–45 minutes. Cool 5–10
    minutes before cutting. Trim ends of strudels, cutting diagonally. Cut
    strudels diagonally into halves. Arrange on plates. Serve with Herb-
    Tomato Sauce (see pg. 32).

Nutritional Data

PER SERVING		EXCHANGES	
Calories:	236	Milk:	0.0
% Calories from fat:	17	Vegetable:	4.0
Fat (gm):	4.8	Fruit:	0.5
Sat. fat (gm):	0.7	Bread:	1.0
Cholesterol (mg):	0	Meat:	0.0
Sodium (mg):	87	Fat:	1.0
Protein (gm):	5.7		
Carbohydrate (gm):	41.9		

INDEX